THE ALASKA
WILD BERRY
COOKBOOK

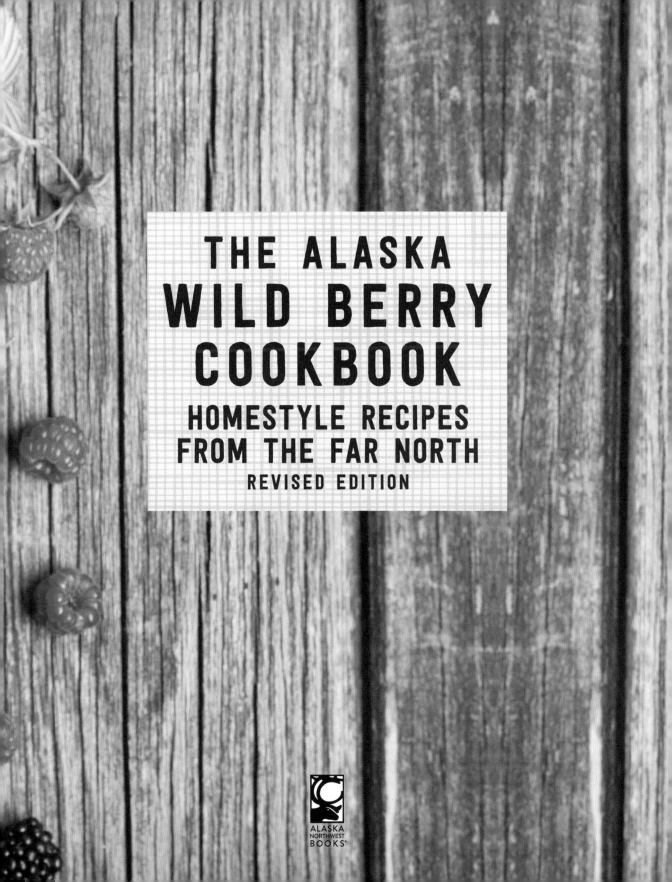

THE ALASKA
WILD BERRY
COOKBOOK

HOMESTYLE RECIPES
FROM THE FAR NORTH

REVISED EDITION

ALASKA
NORTHWEST
BOOKS®

CONTENTS

FOREWORD

Nature provides us with no more delicious, nourishing, or prolific food than the berries that grow in wild abandon throughout our Northern landscape. Wild berries have been an important part of the Native American diet and tradition for centuries. Many people have formed traditions of their own with yearly outings to pick berries of all kinds, both wild and cultivated, to use in jams, jellies, preserves, and pies.

In recent years, more and more people have become aware of the substantial health benefits from the wide varieties of berries that grow in the wild and that are available from grocery stores. Strawberries, loganberries, currants, gooseberries, lingonberries, bilberries, and more are healthful sources of vitamin C, calcium, magnesium, potassium, phytochemicals, and flavonoids.

Wild berry picking is an enjoyable and time-honored tradition, especially in Alaska. Nearly 50 species of berries grow wild in Alaska. Most of these berries are edible, many a real treat to the taste buds. Some, however, are inedible or even poisonous. Whenever picking berries in the wild, it is a good idea to take along a reliable identification guide so that you know exactly what you are picking. When picking wild berries, or any wild plant, for consumption, avoid any that seem questionable.

Berry picking is a wonderful family project—and so is eating the bounty. For the less adventurous, more and more wild berries and cultivated berries are available at grocery stores, farmer's markets, food co-ops, and "u-pick'em" farms. This book presents a choice selection of over two hundred recipes that range far and beyond the usual sampling of pies, toppings, and jams. Besides desserts, you'll find recipes for beverages, marinades and meat dishes, stuffings, candies, sauces, trail foods, and even cocktails. Also included is invaluable information on a multitude of ways to preserve berries. And if berry picking isn't your thing, or if you live in an area where the more unusual varieties are not available, cultivated varieties can be substituted for most of the wild berries in the recipes.

–The Editors

ABOUT BERRIES

In this volume, we have concentrated our recipes among the more abundant or more popular species of wild berries. Many berries native to other regions are similar to ours and can be used in place of the Northern fruit suggested for recipes here. Cultivated species may also be substituted for wild berries, although one must remember that they are often less tart than their wild relatives and adjustments in the sugar added may be necessary.

The different forms of raspberries may be substituted one for the other and blueberries likewise. The red currant is a distinctive fruit, and it is probably best not to use other varieties of currants when a recipe calls for red ones. Lowbush and highbush cranberries are entirely different and require different recipes. For more information on the different types of berries, consult the glossary on page 186.

The farther north you can collect rose hips (fruit of the rose), the more vitamin C content they will have. Rose hips are extremely useful in the North where vitamin C is so lacking and oranges so expensive! They can be used alone or with other fruit. Rose hips should definitely be harvested whenever available. There is difference of opinion about when to harvest. Some people say they should be picked just before the first frost and others prefer to pluck them after the frost.

Many of the recipes given here are in the dessert category, but you may be surprised by how many other ways there are to use wild berries. Lowbush cranberries are particularly good in certain meat dishes and are useful as a marinade for meat. Wild berries are fine for jam and jelly making, of course, not to mention for drying and freezing.

Food preparation often involves a certain amount of experimentation, so do try new combinations and methods and be an experimenter yourself. You may have some delightful eating if you are brave enough to venture making changes in recipes. However you prepare them, wild berries are fun to work with from the time of harvest through the eating. We think you will agree.

BREADS AND BREAKFASTS

BLUEBERRY PAN BISCUITS

Karen Jettmar • Gustavus, Alaska

Vegetable oil, for greasing

1 cup blueberries (huckleberries are good too)

2 cups all-purpose flour

2 teaspoons baking powder

1 teaspoon salt

2 tablespoons vegetable oil

⅔ cup milk

Butter, for serving

Honey, for serving

Grease a large cast-iron skillet (choose one with a lid) and preheat it on top of the stove on low heat. Don't let it get smoking hot.

Mix together the berries, flour, baking powder, and salt in a bowl. Add the oil and milk and mix together until the dough is soft. Do not overmix, or the biscuits will be tough.

Drop the dough by spoonfuls onto the heated skillet. Cover with the lid and keep on low heat, cooking the dough for about 10 minutes on each side, turning once. Serve hot with butter and honey.

MAKES 8 SERVINGS

VARIATION: Blueberry Drop Biscuits: Use the same ingredients (or a biscuit mix), adding 3 tablespoons brown sugar with the dry ingredients. Drop spoonfuls of the dough onto a baking sheet or large cast-iron skillet and bake in a 400°F oven for 15 to 20 minutes.

BERRY-STUFFED BISCUITS

2¼ cups purchased biscuit mix, plus ingredients called for on the package

1 cup walnuts, chopped fine

¼ cup candied orange peel

1 tablespoon dried orange peel, chopped or in granules

½ cup Whole Berry Cranberry Sauce (page 52)

½ cup butter, creamed

Honey, as needed

Prepare the biscuits and bake according to the package directions. Let cool.

For the stuffing mixture: Mix the nuts with the candied and dried orange peels and the cranberry sauce. Blend in the butter, a little at a time, and moisten further with enough honey to make it spreadable. Split the baked biscuits and stuff with the berry mixture.

Wrap the stuffed biscuits in foil and freeze. To be their best, these stuffed biscuits should be made at least 10 days before they will be served.

To serve, preheat the oven to 400°F. Place the foil-wrapped biscuits on a baking sheet, and bake for 6 to 8 minutes. Unwrap the biscuits and bake them for another 2 minutes.

MAKES 8 SERVINGS

VARIATION: Substitute strawberry jam for the cranberry sauce.

JAM BUNS

2 cups all-purpose flour

2 teaspoons baking powder

2 tablespoons sugar

¼ teaspoon salt

1 cup vegetable shortening

1 large egg, slightly beaten

½ cup milk

1 teaspoon vanilla extract

Wild berry jam

Preheat the oven to 375°F. Line a 12-cup muffin pan with paper liners, or grease lightly with vegetable shortening.

Sift together the flour, baking powder, sugar, and salt. Cream the shortening and egg together, then gradually add the milk and vanilla. Slowly mix in the dry ingredients.

Using a rolling pin, roll out the dough on a lightly floured work surface into a 9-by-12-inch rectangle. Using a large knife, cut the dough into 3-inch squares. Drop a spoonful of any wild berry jam onto the center of half the squares. Cover with the remaining squares. Pinch the edges together to seal the buns and place them in the prepared muffin pan.

Bake the buns until well browned, about 15 minutes.

MAKES 12 BUNS

WHOLE WHEAT-BERRY MUFFINS

½ to ¾ cup dried wild berries

1 cup stone-ground, whole wheat flour

½ cup all-purpose flour

½ cup toasted wheat germ

½ cup sugar

1½ teaspoons baking soda

½ teaspoon salt

8 ounces plain yogurt

2 large eggs

¼ cup vegetable oil

Butter, for serving

Preheat the oven to 400°F. Line a 12-cup muffin pan with paper liners, or grease lightly with vegetable oil.

In a bowl, stir together the berries, whole wheat flour, all-purpose flour, wheat germ, sugar, baking soda, and salt. In another bowl, stir together the yogurt, eggs, and oil and pour over the flour mixture. Stir the mixture just enough to moisten the dry ingredients.

Spoon the batter into the prepared muffin pan, filling each cup about three-quarters full. Bake until a toothpick or skewer inserted into the center comes out clean, 18 to 20 minutes.

Serve warm, with lots of butter.

MAKES 12 MUFFINS

BLUEBERRY MUFFINS

Pacific Northwest Blueberry Growers Association

¼ cup butter, softened

2 large eggs, slightly beaten

1 cup sugar

½ teaspoon salt

2 cups all-purpose flour

2 teaspoons baking powder

½ cup milk

1 teaspoon vanilla extract

2 cups fresh, frozen or canned (drained) blueberries

Preheat the oven to 350°F. Line a 12-cup muffin pan with paper liners, or grease lightly with butter.

In a bowl, beat together the butter, eggs, sugar, and salt. Sift the flour and baking powder together. Gradually beat the flour mixture, alternating with the milk, into the butter mixture. Stir in the vanilla and the blueberries.

Spoon the batter into the prepared muffin pan, dividing evenly. Bake until a toothpick or skewer inserted into the center of a muffin comes out clean, about 25 minutes.

MAKES 12 MUFFINS

LOWBUSH CRANBERRY MUFFINS

University of Alaska Cooperative Extension Service

¾ cup lowbush cranberries

¾ cup powdered sugar

2 cups all-purpose flour

¼ cup sugar

3 teaspoons baking powder

1 scant teaspoon salt

1 cup milk

1 large egg, well-beaten

4 tablespoons vegetable shortening, melted

Preheat the oven to 350°F. Line a 12-cup muffin pan with paper liners, or grease lightly with vegetable shortening.

Mix the cranberries with the powdered sugar and let the mixture stand while preparing the muffin batter. Sift together the flour, sugar, baking powder, and salt. Add the milk, egg, and melted shortening. Stir just until the dry ingredients are moistened. Gently fold in the sugared cranberries.

Spoon the batter into the prepared muffin pan, filling each cup roughly two-thirds full, and bake until a toothpick or skewer inserted into the center comes out clean, about 20 minutes.

MAKES 12 MUFFINS

SOURDOUGH CRANBERRY MUFFINS

Mary Alice Sanguinetti • Naknek, Alaska

1½ cups unsifted all-purpose flour

½ cup whole wheat flour

¾ cup firmly packed brown sugar

3 tablespoons powdered buttermilk

1 teaspoon salt

1 teaspoon baking soda

½ cup lowbush cranberries

1 large egg, slightly beaten

½ cup orange juice

½ cup vegetable oil

¾ cup thick sourdough starter

Preheat the oven to 375°F. Line a 12-cup muffin pan with paper liners, or grease lightly with vegetable oil.

In a bowl, mix together the all-purpose flour, whole wheat flour, brown sugar, buttermilk powder, salt, and baking soda, and then stir in the cranberries. In a large bowl, mix together the egg, orange juice, and oil. Stir the sourdough starter into the egg mixture. Add the flour mixture to the egg mixture and stir just enough to blend the ingredients.

Spoon the batter into the prepared muffin pan, filling each cup about two-thirds full. Bake until a toothpick or skewer inserted into the center of a muffin comes out clean, 30 to 35 minutes.

MAKES 12 MUFFINS

VARIATIONS:

- Use oatmeal or rye flour instead of whole wheat flour.
- To adjust the sweetness of the muffins, increase the ¾ cup brown sugar to 1 cup or decrease to ½ cup.

BLUEBERRY PANCAKES

2 cups purchased dry
pancake mix

2 cups milk

1 large egg, slightly beaten

2 tablespoons butter, melted

1 cup blueberries, drained

Vegetable oil or shortening,
for cooking

1 tablespoon sugar, optional

2 teaspoons ground
cinnamon, optional

Butter, optional

Maple syrup, optional

Put the pancake mix in a bowl. Add the milk, egg, and melted butter to the pancake mix and stir gently. Fold the drained blueberries into the batter.

Cook the pancakes on a hot, greased griddle or frying pan, turning them once so that they brown evenly on each side.

To serve, mix the sugar and cinnamon together and sprinkle on the pancakes, or top with butter and maple syrup.

MAKES 8 TO 10 SERVINGS

Lowbush cranberries or blueberries may be stored in rigid containers filled to overflowing with cold water and covered. In cold weather, these berries may be poured into cloth bags and stored out of doors. Hang them up on nails to keep the pests away. Allow them to freeze and, kept frozen, they will keep all winter this way.

DANISH PANCAKES

FRUIT SAUCE
½ **lemon**

½ **orange**

1 **apple, peeled, cored, and sliced**

2 **cups lowbush cranberries**

1½ **cups maple syrup**

PANCAKES
1½ **cups all-purpose flour, sifted**

2 **tablespoons sugar**

1 **teaspoon salt**

½ **teaspoon ground cardamom**

4 **large eggs, beaten**

1⅔ **cups milk, room temperature**

½ **cup butter, melted**

For best results, the fruit sauce should be made the day before this dish is to be served. To make the sauce, first remove the seeds from the lemon and orange. Combine the lemon, orange, apple slices, and cranberries in the bowl of a food processor and process until finely chopped. Add the syrup and process again until the mixture is well combined. Store in the refrigerator.

The next day, prepare the pancake batter: Sift together the flour, sugar, salt, and cardamom. In a bowl, combine the eggs, milk, and butter. Add the egg mixture to the flour mixture, beating until smooth.

To bake, spread 3 to 4 tablespoons of the batter onto a hot, ungreased griddle to make a 6-inch-round pancake. Flip each pancake once to cook evenly on both sides. Once it is cooked, remove each pancake from the griddle and fold it in half and then half again, to form a fan shape. Place the pancakes on a wire rack and keep them warm in a low oven until ready to serve.

To serve, warm the prepared fruit sauce in a saucepan over low heat until bubbling, and then drizzle over the top of the pancakes.

MAKES 6 TO 8 SERVINGS

SNOWFLAKE PANCAKES WITH BLUEBERRIES

Lucille Preston • Kelso, Washington

¼-ounce package dry yeast

¼ cup warm water

1 quart buttermilk

4 tablespoons sugar

1 tablespoon baking soda

1 teaspoon salt

4 cups all-purpose flour

2 tablespoons baking powder

¼ cup vegetable oil, plus more for greasing

6 large eggs, well-beaten

1 cup blueberries

The preparation of these pancakes must begin the night before they are to be served. In a small bowl, stir the yeast into warm water until dissolved. In a separate bowl, mix together the buttermilk, sugar, baking soda, and salt. Add the yeast mixture to the buttermilk mixture. Sift the flour and baking powder together. Add the flour mixture and the ¼ cup oil to the buttermilk mixture. Mix well. Fold in the eggs. Refrigerate the batter overnight in a container large enough to allow it to double in bulk. The batter will keep in the refrigerator for up to a week.

Immediately before cooking, add the blueberries to the batter and stir gently just to combine. Cook the pancakes on a hot, greased griddle or frying pan, flipping once to ensure they are evenly browned on both sides.

Serve warm.

MAKES 10 SERVINGS

SWEDISH PANCAKES

Prepared pancake batter (a purchased packaged mix or your own favorite recipe)

Vegetable oil or shortening, for greasing

Canned lowbush cranberries or Lowbush Cranberry Sauce (page 50)

Powdered sugar, for sprinkling

For each tiny pancake, pour 2 teaspoons of the pancake batter onto a hot, greased griddle or frying pan, flipping once to ensure even browning. Keep warm in a low oven while you cook the rest of the batter.

To serve, arrange 6 of the little pancakes around the edge of a plate and place a dab of lowbush cranberries or cranberry sauce on each. Sprinkle with powdered sugar and serve right away.

SERVINGS VARY

WILD BERRY CRÊPES

2 large eggs

1 cup milk, plus more if needed

1 cup all-purpose flour

½ teaspoon salt

Nonstick cooking spray, for greasing

Softened butter, optional

Raspberry or strawberry jam, slightly warmed

In a large bowl, beat the eggs slightly, then add the milk, flour, and salt. Stir the batter until it is smooth and evenly blended. Cover the bowl and allow to stand for 1 hour.

The batter should be extremely thin—just thick enough to coat a spoon dipped into it. Stir in a little more milk if necessary. Grease a small frying pan (5 to 6 inches in diameter) and place over medium heat. Pour in just enough batter to thinly cover the bottom of the pan. If there is a little too much batter in the pan, pour it back into the bowl, leaving a coating of batter in the pan. Cook on one side over moderate heat until lightly browned; turn with a spatula and cook on the other side until lightly browned. Transfer the crêpe to a plate and immediately spread a little butter, if desired, and jam over the surface, then roll it up or fold it into quarters.

Put the filled crêpe into a low oven to keep warm, and continue to cook and fill the remaining crêpes. These are best served warm.

MAKES 8 SERVINGS

VARIATION: Raspberry Crêpes: Add ⅛ salt to the batter. Add 1 tablespoon of brandy to the raspberry jam. To serve, lightly sprinkle the finished crêpes with powdered sugar.

CRANBERRY NUT BREAD

Nonstick cooking spray,
for greasing

4 cups all-purpose flour, plus
more as needed

2 cups sugar

3 teaspoons baking powder

1 teaspoon baking soda

1½ teaspoons salt

2 oranges

4 tablespoons butter, melted

2 large eggs, well-beaten

4 cups lowbush cranberries

1½ cups chopped nuts

Preheat the oven to 350°F. Grease and flour two 5-by-9-inch loaf pans.

In a bowl, sift together the 4 cups flour, the sugar, baking powder, baking soda, and salt, leaving a well in the middle of the mixture. Grate the zest from the oranges and set aside. Squeeze the juice from the oranges into a large measuring cup and combine with the butter, eggs, and reserved zest. Add enough water to make a total of 1½ cups. Pour the orange juice mixture into the well of the flour mixture and stir just enough to completely dampen the dry ingredients. Fold in the cranberries and nuts.

Pour the batter into the prepared loaf pans, dividing evenly (they will be about two-thirds full) and bake until it springs back to the touch, 40 to 60 minutes, depending upon the size of pans used. Let cool before serving.

This bread is even better after it has been frozen for a few weeks.

MAKES 2 LOAVES

VARIATIONS:

- Substitute whole wheat flour for half of the white flour.
- Substitute 1 cup candied orange peel for 1 cup of the berries.
- Add 1 teaspoon ground nutmeg, ½ teaspoon ground allspice or cloves, or some of each.
- Substitute dried wild berries for half of the cranberries.

SPICED CRANBERRY BREAD

Betty Ryan • Seattle, Washington

2 large oranges

6 tablespoons butter

2¾ cups all-purpose flour

2 cups sugar

1 cup whole wheat flour

1 teaspoon salt

1 teaspoon baking soda

1½ teaspoons baking powder

1 teaspoon ground cinnamon

1 teaspoon ground nutmeg

½ teaspoon ground allspice

½ teaspoon ground ginger

½ teaspoon ground cloves

2 large eggs, slightly beaten

2 cups coarsely chopped walnuts

3 cups frozen lowbush cranberries

This is an excellent holiday bread, but it should be made at least a month before using. It is better when allowed to "ripen" in the freezer for a few weeks. Preheat the oven to 325°F. Line two 4½-by-8½-inch or 5-by-9-inch loaf pans with strips of foil to fit.

Grate the zest from the oranges and set aside. Juice the oranges and add enough water to make 1¾ cups total liquid. Pour into a saucepan. Add the butter and reserved zest to the orange juice mixture and bring to a boil. Set the orange juice mixture aside to cool.

Into a bowl, sift together 2½ cups of the all-purpose flour, the sugar, whole wheat flour, salt, baking soda, baking powder, cinnamon, nutmeg, allspice, ginger, and cloves. Make a well in the center of the flour mixture. Pour the cooled orange juice mixture and eggs into the well and stir until the dry ingredients are moistened. Stir in the chopped nuts.

Remove the cranberries from the freezer at the last minute and spread quickly on a baking sheet. Toss the berries with the remaining ¼ cup flour before the berries have a chance to thaw. Stir the floured berries into the batter quickly but gently, being careful not to break the fruit. Fill the prepared loaf pans with the batter, dividing evenly. Bake until a toothpick or skewer inserted into the center comes out clean, 45 minutes to 1½ hours, depending on the size of the pans. Be sure to test for doneness since this bread is easy to underbake.

Allow the baked bread to cool on racks for 20 minutes. Remove the cooled bread from the pans and peel off the foil. Cool the loaves completely before wrapping them in foil and freezing. This bread will slice without crumbling if kept in the freezer until just before serving.

MAKES 2 LOAVES

VARIATIONS:

- Stir ½ to 1 cup chopped candied orange peel into the batter before baking.
- Substitute 1 cup firmly packed brown sugar for 1 cup of the white sugar.

COFFEE BREAK CAKE

Corrine U. Palmer • Olympia, Washington

Nonstick cooking spray, for greasing

2 cups purchased biscuit mix, plus ingredients called for on package instructions

Lowbush cranberries

1 cup sugar

Preheat the oven to 325°F and grease an 8-inch square baking pan.

Prepare the biscuit mix according to directions on the package. Turn the batter into the prepared pan and cover with a layer of berries. Sprinkle the sugar over the berries. Bake until golden brown, 20 to 25 minutes. Serve hot or cold, plain or with a topping. This is a good recipe when you have only a few berries on hand.

MAKES 8 SERVINGS

VARIATION: Almost any firm, small-seeded berry will work in this recipe.

CRAN-APPLE BREAKFAST TREAT

Nonstick cooking spray, for greasing

2 cups all-purpose flour

3 tablespoons sugar

3 teaspoons baking powder

Pinch of salt

1 cup heavy cream

1 large egg, slightly beaten

Lowbush Cranberry Jelly (page 174)

2 to 3 apples, peeled and cut into thick slices

Brown sugar

Ground cinnamon

Butter

Preheat the oven to 400°F and grease a 9-inch square baking pan.

Sift together the flour, sugar, baking powder, and salt. Whip the cream until thick and carefully stir in the egg. Add the whipped cream and egg to the flour mixture and gently stir until the dough forms a ball.

Press the dough evenly into the prepared pan and cover it with a thick layer of jelly. Arrange the apple slices in rows on top of the jelly and press firmly into place. Sprinkle with brown sugar and cinnamon. Dot generously with butter. Bake until golden brown, 30 to 35 minutes. Serve warm.

MAKES 6 TO 8 SERVINGS

LOWBUSH CRANBERRY COFFEE CAKE

University of Alaska Cooperative Extension Service

Nonstick cooking spray, for greasing

2¼ cups all-purpose flour

1 cup sugar

3 teaspoons baking powder

¾ teaspoon salt

8 tablespoons butter

1 large egg, slightly beaten

½ cup milk

2½ cups lowbush cranberries

Preheat the oven to 375°F. Grease an 8-inch square baking pan.

Sift together 2 cups of the flour, ½ cup of the sugar, the baking powder, and the salt. Cut 5 tablespoons of the butter into the dry ingredients until the mixture is crumbly. Mix the egg and milk, and then add it to the flour mixture, stirring slowly, then beat until well blended. Spread the batter into the prepared pan and sprinkle the berries evenly over the top.

For the streusel topping, combine the remaining ¼ cup flour and ½ cup sugar, and then cut the remaining 3 tablespoons butter into the mixture until crumbly. Sprinkle this over the berries. Bake until a toothpick or skewer inserted into the center comes out clean, 30 to 35 minutes. Serve warm.

MAKES 6 TO 8 SERVINGS

Use an electric fan to quickly clean your picked berries. Set up the fan outdoors and place a large container in front of and below it. Slowly pour the berries from above the fan so they fall through the moving air and into the container. Leaves and debris will be blown away.

NORTH STAR SCONES

FILLING

¾ cup wild berry jelly or jam

½ cup finely chopped apple

3 tablespoons brown sugar

½ teaspoon ground cinnamon

¼ cup chopped walnuts

DOUGH

2 cups all-purpose flour

4 teaspoons baking powder

1 tablespoon sugar

Pinch of salt

5 tablespoons butter

Beaten egg white or milk, for brushing

Coarse sugar, for sprinkling

Preheat the oven to 450°F.

Prepare the filling by combining the jelly, chopped apple, brown sugar, cinnamon, and nuts. Blend lightly until the mixture becomes a spreadable consistency.

For the dough, in separate bowl, sift together the flour, baking powder, sugar, and salt. Cut in the butter until the mixture is crumbly. Roll out the dough on parchment paper into a 10-by-20-inch rectangle. Spread the filling over half of the dough, starting from a short end, then carefully fold the other half of the dough over the filling. Press the edges firmly together with a floured fork.

Transfer the scone to an ungreased baking sheet, parchment paper all. Trim off the excess paper and brush the top of the scone with egg white or milk then sprinkle lightly with coarse sugar. Bake until golden brown, 20 to 25 minutes. Cut into squares and serve warm.

MAKES 8 SCONES

QUICK COFFEE CAKE

4 tablespoons butter, softened, plus more for greasing

¾ cup sugar

1 large egg

½ cup milk

½ teaspoon almond extract

1½ cups all-purpose flour

2 teaspoons baking powder

¼ teaspoon salt

½ cup wild berry jam

½ cup finely chopped pecans

Preheat the oven to 350°F and grease an 8-inch square baking pan.

In a bowl, combine the butter and sugar and beat until fluffy. Beat in the egg, followed by the milk and almond extract. In another bowl, mix together the flour, baking powder, and salt. Add the flour mixture to the egg-butter mixture and mix just until blended.

Spread the batter into the prepared pan. Place dollops of your favorite jam (wild strawberry is very good) over the top. Sprinkle with the chopped pecans. Bake until a toothpick or skewer inserted into the center comes out clean, about 30 minutes.

MAKES 6 TO 8 SERVINGS

BLUEBERRY BREAKFAST CAKE

Anna Marie Davis • Anchorage, Alaska

Nonstick cooking spray, for greasing

1½ cups all-purpose flour

2 teaspoons baking powder

¾ cup sugar

½ teaspoon salt

⅔ cup milk

¼ cup plus 3 tablespoons butter, melted

1½ teaspoons vanilla extract

2 teaspoons finely grated lemon zest

1 large egg

1½ cups wild blueberries

½ cup firmly packed brown sugar

Preheat the oven to 350°F. Grease an 8- or 9-inch square baking pan.

In a bowl, combine the flour, baking powder, sugar, and salt. Add the milk, ¼ cup of the melted butter, the vanilla, and 1 teaspoon of the lemon zest. Mix well with a wooden spoon. Add the egg and mix thoroughly. Spoon the batter into the prepared pan.

In a bowl, mix together the berries, brown sugar, remaining 3 tablespoons of the melted butter, and 1 teaspoon of lemon zest. Drizzle this mixture over the batter in the pan. Bake until a toothpick or skewer inserted into the center comes out clean, about 40 minutes. Let cool and cut into squares to serve.

MAKES 6 TO 8 SERVINGS

Gather wild berries in the afternoon of a sunny day if you can. Several hours of exposure to the sun before picking means more ascorbic acid (vitamin C) in the fruit. It is also better than picking earlier when there is still dew on the plants. The berries will be wet and so will you if they are picked under those conditions.

BLUEBERRY UPSIDE-DOWN ROLLS

Vegetable shortening,
for greasing

¾ cup sugar

½ cup orange juice

¼ cup plus 1 tablespoon
butter

2 teaspoons finely grated
orange zest

½ cup chopped nuts

1 cup blueberries

2 cups all-purpose flour

3 teaspoons baking powder

½ teaspoon salt

3 to 4 tablespoons
vegetable shortening

¾ cup milk

Ground cinnamon,
for sprinkling

Preheat the oven to 450°F and thoroughly grease a 12-cup muffin pan.

In a saucepan, combine ½ cup of the sugar with the orange juice, ¼ cup of the butter, and the orange zest and cook for 2 minutes. Pour the mixture into the prepared muffin pan, dividing evenly. Sprinkle the nuts and then the berries evenly onto the sugar mixture.

Sift together the flour, baking powder, and salt. Cut the shortening into the mixture until crumbly. Add the milk and stir until the dough follows the spoon around the bowl. Turn the dough onto a lightly floured work surface and knead for 15 seconds. Using a rolling pin, roll out the dough into ¼-inch-thick rectangle.

Melt the remaining 1 tablespoon of butter and brush it onto the dough. Sprinkle the top with the remaining ¼ cup sugar and the cinnamon. Roll the dough up lengthwise as you would for a jellyroll. Cut the roll crosswise into 1-inch slices and place each slice, cut side down, over the mix in the muffin pans. Bake until a toothpick or skewer inserted into the center comes out clean, 20 to 25 minutes.

Remove the rolls from the oven and let cool slightly on a wire rack. Run a knife around the edge of the pan to loosen the rolls and topping, then carefully invert the rolls, topping side up, onto a platter. Serve warm.

MAKES 12 ROLLS

MAIN DISHES

Sweet and Tangy Glazed Chicken **34**

Wild Game Patties with
    Berry Sauce **34**

Meatloaf with Cranberry Ketchup **35**

Cranberry Meatballs with
    Mushroom Sauce **36**

Raspberry–Rose Hips Pork Chops **37**

Baked Easter Ham **38**

Brown Sugar Ham with Sweet Potatoes
    and Dried Berries **39**

Glazed Spareribs **40**

Cranberry-Glazed Moose **41**

SWEET AND TANGY GLAZED CHICKEN

⅔ cup Lowbush Cranberry Juice (page 160)

½ cup prepared mustard

½ cup honey

¼ cup butter, melted

2 frying chickens, cut into serving pieces

In a bowl, stir together the Lowbush Cranberry Juice, mustard, honey, and butter.

Place the chicken pieces on a broiling pan and brush with the juice mixture. Broil 6 to 8 inches from the heat, turning and basting with juice as necessary, until tender and cooked through, 40 to 60 minutes.

Serve warm.

MAKES 6 TO 8 SERVINGS

WILD GAME PATTIES WITH BERRY SAUCE

1½ pounds ground game meat or beef

4 tablespoons butter

Pinch of dried rosemary

Dash of Worcestershire sauce

½ teaspoon dry mustard

5 or 6 tablespoons Lowbush Cranberry Juice (page 160)

Form the ground game meat or beef into oblong patties about ¾-inch thick. Melt 3 tablespoons of the butter in a large skillet. Add the rosemary. Place the patties in the butter and cook to desired doneness, and then transfer to a hot platter.

Add the remaining 1 tablespoon butter and the Worcestershire sauce to the butter in the skillet. Stir in the dry mustard and the cranberry juice. Heat, but do not boil. When hot, pour over the burger steaks on the platter. Serve warm.

MAKES 6 SERVINGS

MEATLOAF WITH CRANBERRY KETCHUP

2 large eggs

1½ cups soft bread crumbs

1 cup chopped onion

¼ cup chopped
green bell pepper

1 pound ground moose or
caribou meat

1 pound lean, ground pork

¼ cup Highbush Cranberry
Ketchup (page 55)

¼ cup milk

2 teaspoons prepared
horseradish

1 teaspoon dry mustard

¾ teaspoon salt

1 cup cranberry sauce

Preheat the oven to 375°F. Beat the eggs in a large bowl; stir in the bread crumbs, onion, and green bell pepper. Gently mix in the meat and pork. In another bowl, mix together the Highbush Cranberry Ketchup, milk, horseradish, mustard, and salt; add this to the first mixture.

Shape the meat mixture into a round loaf and place on a sheet of foil in a shallow pan. Bake until well browned and crusty, about 45 minutes. A few minutes before the dish is finished baking, drain the cranberry sauce and spread over the loaf.

Cut the meatloaf into slices and serve warm.

MAKES 6 SERVINGS

CRANBERRY MEATBALLS WITH MUSHROOM SAUCE

1 cup soft bread crumbs

½ to ¾ cup crushed lowbush cranberries

½ cup tomato sauce

2 large eggs, slightly beaten

2 pounds ground beef

½ to ¾ cup quick-cooking rice

¼ cup finely chopped onion

1 teaspoon salt

¼ teaspoon freshly ground black pepper

Whole wheat flour, for dredging

Vegetable oil, for frying

1 (10¾-ounce) can mushroom soup

Milk or water

Preheat the oven to 350°F. Place the bread crumbs in a large bowl; add the berries, tomato sauce, and eggs. Stir to mix and let stand until crumbs are well moistened. Mix in the ground beef, rice, onion, salt, and pepper. Form good-sized meatballs and roll them in whole wheat flour.

Heat the shortening in an oven-proof skillet and add the meatballs in batches, cooking them until browned on all sides. Dilute the mushroom soup by half with milk or water, then pour over the meatballs. Cover and bake in the oven for 30 minutes. Turn the meatballs and cook for another 15 minutes uncovered.

Serve warm.

MAKES 8 SERVINGS

RASPBERRY-ROSE HIPS PORK CHOPS

1 teaspoon ground ginger

1 teaspoon salt

½ teaspoon freshly ground black pepper

1 teaspoon paprika

¼ cup all-purpose flour

6 thick-cut pork chops

1 tablespoon vegetable shortening

½ cup Rose Hip Juice (page 160)

½ cup raspberry juice

2 teaspoons vinegar

1 tablespoon brown sugar

2 medium-sized tomatoes, sliced

Mix together the ginger, salt, pepper, paprika, pepper, and flour in a paper bag. Drop the pork chops into the bag and shake well to coat all sides with the flour mixture. Heat the shortening in a skillet and brown the chops on all sides.

Mix the fruit juices together and add the vinegar; pour this mixture over the pork chops. Sprinkle on the sugar, cover the skillet, and simmer the chops slowly until they are tender, about 45 minutes. Serve with a tomato slice on top of each. The tomatoes may be broiled if you wish.

MAKES 6 SERVINGS

BAKED EASTER HAM

1 bone-in ham, 6 to 8 pounds

1 cup lowbush cranberry or
other berry syrup or jelly

1 teaspoon ground cloves

1 teaspoon ground nutmeg

1 teaspoon ground allspice

1 teaspoon dry mustard

½ teaspoon freshly ground
black pepper

½ cup orange juice

2 tablespoons dried
orange granules or finely
grated orange zest

½ cup hot water

Preheat the oven to 325°F.

Remove the skin and trim any excess fat from the ham. Using a sharp knife, carefully cut holes into the ham 2 inches from one another and as deep as the bone. Do this on all sides.

In a pot, bring the syrup or jelly, cloves, nutmeg, allspice, dry mustard, pepper, orange juice, dried orange granules or zest, and hot water to boil together to form a syrup. Pour 1 tablespoon of this hot syrup into each hole in the ham, then place the ham in a large roasting bag. Place the bag into a roasting pan. Pour half the remaining syrup over the ham, then close the bag, piercing several small holes in its upper side. Bake for 18 minutes for each pound of ham.

Brown the meat by slitting open the bag 30 minutes before it's through cooking. Pour the remaining syrup over the ham and finish baking. Serve warm.

MAKES 10 TO 12 SERVINGS

BROWN SUGAR HAM WITH SWEET POTATOES AND DRIED BERRIES

1½ pounds boneless, center-cut ham

1 cup dried serviceberries

3 medium-sized sweet potatoes or yams

Freshly ground black pepper

1 cup brown sugar

2 cups milk

Preheat the oven to 350°F. Place the ham in a baking dish and cover with dried serviceberries. Peel the sweet potatoes, cut them lengthwise, and add to the ham and berries. Sprinkle lightly with pepper and the brown sugar.

In a saucepan, warm the milk over medium heat, watching carefully, until it just starts to come to a boil. Immediately remove the pan from the heat, then pour the hot milk into the baking dish. Cover and bake for 1 hour.

Remove the cover and bake for another 30 minutes to brown the potatoes. Serve warm.

MAKES 4 SERVINGS

GLAZED SPARERIBS

Alaska Wild Berry Trails

1 rack of pork spareribs

Salt and pepper

Chopped fresh sage or thyme

2 cups boiling water

1 (8-ounce can) tomato sauce or paste

1 cup Lowbush Cranberry Juice (page 160)

Preheat the oven to 400°F. Place the spareribs in a shallow roasting pan and sprinkle with salt, pepper, and sage or thyme. Add the boiling water and bake the ribs for 1 hour.

Drain off the liquid from the pan. In a small bowl, stir together the tomato sauce, cranberry juice, and a pinch of salt. Pour this glaze over the ribs, making sure that the whole rack is completely coated. Reduce the oven heat to 350°F and bake until the ribs are very tender, about 1 hour. Turn the ribs at least once and baste several times with the pan juices.

Cut the rack into individual ribs and serve warm.

MAKES 3 TO 4 SERVINGS

CRANBERRY-GLAZED MOOSE

Alaska Wild Berry Trails

4 pounds moose round or rump

1½ cups cranberry or currant jelly

2 onions, sliced

3 large carrots, diced

2 tablespoons chopped fresh parsley

1 tablespoon salt

½ teaspoon freshly ground black pepper

Place the meat in a large glass or ceramic bowl and add the jelly, onions, carrots, parsley, salt, and pepper. Cover and allow to stand in the refrigerator overnight.

The following day, remove the moose from the liquid and, if you wish, strain out the vegetables. Return the meat to the liquid, add more water if necessary, and proceed using your favorite recipes for pot roast.

Taste the liquid and add more seasoning if you think it needs it. Do not thicken this gravy; it is better thin.

MAKES 8 SERVINGS

When making jelly or jam, it is good to use a large kettle because the liquid increases greatly in bulk as it boils. It may boil over and create an unholy mess if the saucepan is too small.

MARINADES, SAUCES, AND STUFFINGS

MARINADE FOR FLANK STEAK

½ cup Lowbush Cranberry
Juice (page 160)

½ cup minced fresh chives

¼ cup water

3 tablespoons prepared
mustard

2 tablespoons honey

1 tablespoon soy sauce

1 teaspoon salt

½ teaspoon freshly ground
black pepper

½ teaspoon garlic powder

½ teaspoon dill seed

In a large flat dish, mix together the cranberry juice, chives, water, mustard, honey, soy, salt, pepper, garlic powder, and dill seed. Marinate the flank steak in the mixture for 3 hours in the refrigerator, turning several times during the process.

MAKES ENOUGH FOR 1 TO 2 POUNDS OF MEAT

MARINADE FOR FRUITS

½ cup Lowbush Cranberry
Juice (page 160)

¼ cup orange juice

¼ cup blueberry or
raspberry juice

¼ cup maple or corn syrup

¼ cup brandy or fruit liqueur,
optional

Finely grated zest and juice
of 1 lemon

Seeds scraped from
1 vanilla bean, or
¼ teaspoon anise seed

In a bowl, mix together the cranberry, orange, and berry juices; maple syrup; brandy; lemon zest and juice; and vanilla or anise seeds. Pour the mixture over fresh fruits that have been peeled and then sliced, diced, or quartered as needed. Carefully mix the fruit and marinade. Cover and refrigerate for several hours.

MAKES ENOUGH FOR 6 CUPS DICED FRUITS

MARINADE FOR GAME

½ cup Lowbush Cranberry
Juice (page 160)

½ cup vinegar

2 garlic cloves, finely minced

2 tablespoons salt

Cold water enough to
cover meat

In a bowl large enough to hold the marinade and game, mix together the cranberry juice, vinegar, garlic, salt, and water. Soak the game overnight in the refrigerator. Use for any game, including game birds.

MAKES ENOUGH FOR 1 TO 2 POUNDS GAME

MARINADE FOR MOOSE

2 cups Lowbush Cranberry
Juice (page 160)

1 cup olive oil

2 large onions, sliced

2 carrots, sliced

2 garlic cloves, smashed

2 tablespoons dried parsley

1 teaspoon salt

¼ teaspoon dried thyme

8 peppercorns

8 crushed juniper berries

1 whole clove

1 bay leaf

In a bowl large enough to hold the marinade and meat, mix together the cranberry juice, oil, onions, carrots, garlic, parsley, salt, thyme, peppercorns, juniper berries, clove, and bay leaf. Marinate the moose in the refrigerator overnight, the longer the better, turning the meat occasionally.

MAKES ENOUGH FOR 2 TO 4 POUNDS MOOSE

MARINADE FOR SPARERIBS

1½ cups Lowbush Cranberry Juice (page 160)

½ cup tomato puree

½ cup honey

¼ cup tarragon vinegar

1 large onion, chopped

2 cloves garlic, peeled and smashed

2 tablespoons Worcestershire sauce

1 tablespoon prepared mustard

2 teaspoons chili powder

2 teaspoons dried oregano

2 teaspoons salt

Dash of Tabasco sauce

In a large, flat dish, mix together the cranberry juice, tomato puree, honey, vinegar, onion, garlic, Worcestershire, mustard, chili powder, oregano, salt, and Tabasco. Marinate the spareribs in the mixture for 24 hours in the refrigerator, turning frequently. You can also use the marinade for basting the ribs as they cook up to 5 minutes before the ribs are done.

MAKES ENOUGH FOR 5 TO 6 POUNDS RIBS

BAR-B-Q SAUCE

1 cup Lowbush Cranberry Juice (page 160)

1 cup ketchup

½ cup water

¼ cup Worcestershire sauce

1 large tomato, chopped

¼ to ½ green bell pepper, chopped

2 tablespoons minced onion

1 tablespoon prepared horseradish

1½ teaspoons dry mustard

In a saucepan, combine the Lowbush Cranberry Juice, ketchup, water, Worcestershire sauce, tomato, green bell pepper, onion, horseradish, and dry mustard. Simmer over low heat, stirring occasionally, until smooth and hot, about 10 minutes or so. This makes a good barbecue basting sauce for wild game, beef, lamb, or pork.

MAKES ABOUT 3 CUPS

CRANBERRY-HORSERADISH SAUCE

1 cup Lowbush Cranberry Juice (page 160)

1 cup boiling water

½ cup sugar

¼ cup orange juice

1 tablespoon prepared horseradish

1 tablespoon prepared mustard

In a saucepan, combine the Lowbush Cranberry Juice, boiling water, and sugar and boil for 3 minutes. Add the orange juice and boil 2 minutes more. When the mixture has cooled, gently stir in the horseradish and mustard. This is an excellent sauce for serving with ham. (Leave out the horseradish and mustard, and you have a hotcake syrup or dessert sauce.) It's best when served warm.

MAKES ABOUT 2 CUPS

The two "cranberries" you find in Alaska—lowbush cranberries and highbush cranberries—are different from the fruit you typically find on the Thanksgiving table in the lower forty-eight. Also called lingonberries, lowbush cranberries are so named because they grow on close-to-the-ground, small-leafed, bushy plants. Highbush cranberries grow on taller shrubs with relatively large, maplelike leaves. Both types of berries are nutrient-dense and very acidic, boasting high levels of antioxidants.

CITRUS-ALMOND CRANBERRY SAUCE

2 cups sugar

1 cup water

1 pound lowbush cranberries

½ cup orange marmalade

Juice of 1½ lemons

½ cup slivered blanched almonds

Mix the sugar and water in a large saucepan and bring to a boil without stirring. Simmer for 5 minutes, then add the cranberries. Stir thoroughly and cook for at least 3 minutes (or until all the berries have popped their skins) but no longer than 5 minutes. Remove from heat and add the marmalade and lemon juice. Let stand until completely cool. Stir in the almonds. Serve well chilled.

MAKES 2½ TO 3 CUPS

DRIED BERRY SAUCE

1 cup water

1 cup brown sugar

1 tablespoon cornstarch

⅛ teaspoon ground cloves

Pinch of salt

½ cup chopped dried berries or rose hips, or a combination

1 tablespoon vinegar

1 tablespoon melted butter

1 teaspoon finely grated lemon zest

Blend water, sugar, cornstarch, cloves, and salt in a saucepan and cook slowly until sugar is dissolved, stirring constantly. Blend in the dried berries, vinegar, butter, and lemon zest. Continue cooking until well heated. This sauce is excellent with baked ham.

MAKES ABOUT 1 CUP

LOWBUSH CRANBERRY SAUCE

4 cups finely chopped lowbush cranberries

3 to 4 cups sugar

1 tablespoon orange juice

1 tablespoon finely grated orange zest or dried orange rind granules

Combine the cranberries, sugar, orange juice, and zest. Allow to stand in a cool place for a day or two, stirring thoroughly every few hours. No further processing is necessary. Put in sterilized jars and cover (do not seal). Store in a cool place or in refrigerator or freezer. If stored in freezer they should be in plastic containers instead of jars. There is so much acid in cranberries that they will keep for many months if stored properly.

MAKES ABOUT 2½ CUPS

SWEET AND SOUR SAUCE

1 (8-ounce) can crushed pineapple

1 green bell pepper, seeded and chopped

2 large tomatoes, chopped

1 scant cup packed dark brown sugar

1 cup white wine vinegar

¾ cup water

½ cup Blueberry Syrup (page 60) or Cranberry Syrup (page 60)

1 tablespoon Worcestershire sauce

1 teaspoon dry mustard

2 tablespoons cornstarch

Combine the pineapple, green bell pepper, tomatoes, sugar, vinegar, ½ cup of the water, berry syrup, Worcestershire sauce, and mustard in a saucepan. Cover and simmer gently for 15 minutes, stirring occasionally. Blend the cornstarch into the remaining ¼ cup water, then stir into the sauce slowly. Simmer until the sauce is thick and smooth.

MAKES ABOUT 2 CUPS

POLISH-STYLE JUNIPER BERRY SAUCE

1½ teaspoons juniper berries

2 tablespoons butter

2 tablespoons whole wheat flour

1 cup beef broth, plus more as needed

½ cup Madeira wine

Pinch of salt

Pinch of freshly ground black pepper

Place the juniper berries between several thicknesses of waxed paper, then use a rolling pin to crush them to a fine texture. In a saucepan, heat the butter until lightly browned. Gradually stir in the flour and cook over low heat, stirring constantly. Add the broth and simmer for 15 to 20 minutes, stirring occasionally. Add the wine, salt, pepper, and crushed juniper berries. Simmer again for 10 minutes or so. (You may need to add a little more broth if the sauce is too thick.) This sauce goes especially well with grouse or ptarmigan.

MAKES ABOUT 1½ CUPS

MEATBALL SAUCE

½ cup Lowbush Cranberry Sauce (page 50)

¼ cup ketchup

¼ teaspoon garlic powder

2 tablespoons butter

Orange juice, optional

In a saucepan, whisk together the Lowbush Cranberry Sauce, ketchup, and garlic powder. Add the butter, then simmer for 5 minutes. Stir in the orange juice, if desired, for a piquant taste. Serve hot. This is excellent as a dipping sauce for tiny cocktail meatballs.

MAKES ABOUT ¾ CUP

WHOLE BERRY CRANBERRY SAUCE

6 cups lowbush cranberries

4 cups sugar

¾ cup water

In a saucepan, combine the cranberries, sugar, and water and bring to a full, rolling boil. Boil until a little of the juice jells on the spoon, approximately 25 minutes. Pour into sterilized jelly glasses and seal.

MAKES 3 TO 4 CUPS

VARIATIONS:

- Substitute ½ cup honey for the same amount of sugar and reduce the amount of water used by 2 tablespoons.
- Add slivered crystallized ginger and/or a bit of finely grated orange zest.
- Substitute a portion of orange juice for an equal amount of water.

CRANBERRY MAYONNAISE

¼ cup Whole Berry Cranberry Sauce (above)

1 teaspoon lemon juice

½ teaspoon finely grated orange zest

½ cup mayonnaise

Crush the berries in the sauce with a fork. Gently blend the sauce, lemon juice, and orange zest into the mayonnaise. This is delicious for ham or smoked turkey sandwiches or salads.

MAKES ABOUT ¾ CUP

FRUIT SALAD DRESSING

½ cup your choice
berry juice

½ cup mayonnaise

Sugar, to taste

Carefully mix the berry juice and mayonnaise or the dressing may curdle. Taste a sample and add sugar to suit your preference. This makes a lighter dressing than pure mayonnaise and is more suitable for fruit salads.

MAKES ABOUT 1 CUP

VARIATION: Creamy Fruit Salad Dressings: Start with 1 cup mayonnaise and blend in any of the following variations for fruit salad dressing:

- 1 cup chopped lowbush cranberries and a few drops of orange juice.
- Raspberry puree to taste.
- 1 cup crushed strawberries, 1 tablespoon powdered sugar, 2 tablespoons lemon or orange juice, and 1 cup whipped cream.
- 6 tablespoons crushed strawberries or raspberries, 4 tablespoons slivered toasted almonds, 2 tablespoons berry juice, and 2 tablespoons white wine.

STRAWBERRY-WHITE WINE DRESSING

¼ cup fresh wild strawberries

¼ cup finely chopped pecans

2 tablespoons white wine

1 cup mayonnaise

Crush the berries and drain off all but two tablespoons of the juice. Stir in the pecans and white wine. Carefully fold the berry mixture into the mayonnaise.

MAKES ABOUT 1½ CUPS

VARIATION: Use raspberries instead of strawberries and replace the pecans with slivered toasted almonds.

HIGHBUSH CRANBERRY KETCHUP

6 pounds highbush
cranberries

1¼ pounds sweet
white onions, chopped

3 cups water

3 cups mild vinegar

6 cups sugar

1 tablespoon ground cloves

1 tablespoon ground
cinnamon

1 tablespoon ground allspice

1 tablespoon salt

2 tablespoons celery salt

1½ teaspoons freshly ground
black pepper

In a saucepan, simmer the berries and onions in the water until soft. Push the mixture through a sieve and return the pulp to the saucepan. Add the vinegar, sugar, cloves, cinnamon, allspice, salt, celery salt, and pepper. Bring to a boil, then reduce heat and cook until thick and ketchuplike in consistency. Stir frequently to keep from sticking. Pour into sterilized canning jars and seal immediately. Process for 5 to 10 minutes in a boiling water bath. Use your Highbush Cranberry Ketchup just like a regular tomato ketchup.

MAKES 6 TO 8 CUPS

CRANLILI

University of Alaska Cooperative Extension Service

2 cups fresh lowbush
cranberries

3 medium-sized onions,
sliced

2 large green bell peppers,
roughly chopped

1 cup cider vinegar

½ cup sugar

2 teaspoons salt

Combine the cranberries, onions, and bell peppers in the bowl of a food processor and process until finely chopped. Transfer the cranberry mixture to a saucepan, stir in the vinegar, sugar, and salt, and simmer slowly to develop the flavors, 20 to 30 minutes. Pack in sterilized canning jars and seal immediately. This sauce is especially good on hot dogs and hamburgers.

MAKES ABOUT 6 CUPS

LOWBUSH CRANBERRY KETCHUP

Anna Marie Davis • Anchorage, Alaska

1 pound lowbush cranberries

½ cup mild vinegar

½ cup water

1 cup brown sugar

1 teaspoon ground cinnamon

½ teaspoon ground cloves

½ teaspoon ground ginger

½ teaspoon paprika

½ teaspoon salt

¼ teaspoon freshly ground
black pepper

2 tablespoons butter

In a saucepan, simmer the berries in the vinegar and water until they are soft. Push the mixture through a sieve and place the pulp in a saucepan. Add the sugar, spices, and salt and cook slowly for 4 or 5 minutes. Add the butter and stir until melted. Pour into sterilized jars, seal, and process for 5 to 10 minutes in a boiling water bath. Serve at room temperature with pork or poultry.

MAKES 1½ TO 2 CUPS

ROSE HIP KETCHUP

1 quart rose hips

2 cups cider vinegar

2 cups sugar

1 teaspoon onion powder

½ teaspoon freshly ground
black pepper

½ teaspoon dry mustard

½ teaspoon salt

½ teaspoon ground cloves

½ teaspoon ground
cinnamon

Pinch of cayenne pepper

Clean the rose hips and place in a saucepan. Barely cover with cold water, then bring to a boil. Simmer until soft, about 15 minutes. Put through a sieve to eliminate all seeds. Add the vinegar, sugar, onion powder, pepper, dry mustard, salt, cloves, cinnamon, and cayenne and return to the saucepan. Cook over medium heat until thick, stirring now and then. Pour into sterilized bottles or canning jars and seal at once. Process for 5 to 10 minutes in a boiling water bath. Use like tomato ketchup.

MAKES 3 TO 4 CUPS

CRANBERRY CHUTNEY

University of Alaska Cooperative Extension Service

2 cups chopped lowbush cranberries

1 cup brown sugar

½ cup seedless raisins

2 tablespoons finely chopped onions

2 tablespoons lemon juice

1 teaspoon salt

In a bowl, mix together the lowbush cranberries, brown sugar, raisins, onions, lemon juice, and salt and mix well. Place in the refrigerator for several hours for flavors to mingle well. Serve with meat.

MAKES 1 TO 1½ CUPS

CRANBERRY DRESSING FOR PORK

¼ cup butter

1 cup diced celery

1 large onion, diced

2 medium-sized apples, peeled and diced

5 cups dried bread cubes

1 teaspoon rubbed sage

¾ teaspoon salt

1 cup Whole Berry Cranberry Sauce (page 52)

¼ cup brown sugar

Finely grated zest of 1 orange

½ cup orange juice

Melt the butter in a large pot and add the celery, onion, and apples. Saute over low heat until softened but not browned. Add the bread cubes, sage, and salt. Place the cranberry sauce, brown sugar, and orange zest in a saucepan and stir over low heat until the sugar is dissolved. Add to the bread mixture. Gradually add the orange juice, mixing until the bread is moistened. This is a good stuffing for crown roast, or it may be baked separately for pork roast.

MAKES 4 TO 6 SERVINGS

CRANBERRY STUFFING

1 cup lowbush cranberries

¼ cup sugar

4 tablespoons butter

½ cup diced ham or bacon

¼ cup chopped celery

2 tablespoons chopped
fresh parsley

3 cups stale bread crumbs

1 cup cornbread crumbs

Poultry seasoning to taste

Run the cranberries and sugar through a food processor until finely chopped. Cook the diced ham, celery, and parsley in butter over low heat until softened but not browned, about 5 minutes. Add the bread and cornbread crumbs, the seasoning, and the chopped cranberry mixture and stir to combine. This is particularly good with baked moose heart, wild duck, or poultry.

MAKES 4 SERVINGS

STUFFING FOR DUCK

3 cups whole wheat bread cubes

½ cup orange juice

½ cup ground lowbush cranberries

⅓ cup orange segments (membrane removed)

2 teaspoons finely grated orange zest

2 cups finely chopped celery

¼ cup melted butter

1 large egg, slightly beaten

¼ teaspoon salt

¼ teaspoon freshly ground black pepper

Toast the bread cubes in the oven to ensure dryness. Add the bread to a bowl with the juice and berries, toss well, and let stand for 15 minutes. Add the orange segments, orange zest, celery, butter, egg, salt, and pepper and toss lightly to mix. Stuff the bird and roast according to your recipe.

MAKES 4 TO 6 SERVINGS

STUFFING FOR GAME BIRDS

Lois Armstrong • Brookings, Oregon

10 slices of Cranberry Nut Bread (page 23)

¾ cup chicken broth

2 tablespoons butter, melted

Salt

Your choice of additional seasonings

1 large egg

Toast the bread slices in a slow oven to ensure dryness. Crumble into a bowl. Add the broth and butter and mix well. Add salt and other seasonings to taste. Mix in the egg. This is an excellent stuffing for any game bird and goose in particular.

MAKES 6 TO 8 SERVINGS

BLUEBERRY SYRUP

Martha Wilson • Toledo, Oregon

4 cups blueberry juice

2 cups sugar

1 to 2 cups corn syrup

Place the juice, sugar, and corn syrup in a saucepan and bring to a boil. Boil for about 3 minutes. The corn syrup will thicken the juice without making it excessively sweet; add more if the berries are very tart. Seal in hot, sterilized canning jars or keep frozen. This is good drizzled on ice cream or hotcakes, stirred into beverages, or poured over puddings.

MAKES 5 TO 6 CUPS

CRANBERRY SYRUP

2 pounds lowbush cranberries

1 cup water

2 cups sugar

½ cup orange juice

In a saucepan, simmer the berries and the water over medium heat until berries soften. Crush the berries with a potato masher and continue cooking slowly for another 10 minutes. Drain overnight in a dampened jelly bag, without squeezing. The pulp may be saved for another use. Add the sugar to the juice, bring to a boil, and boil slowly for 5 minutes. Add the orange juice and boil 1 minute more. Add more sugar to taste. Pour into sterilized canning jars or bottles and seal. This syrup can be used in a variety of ways.

MAKES ABOUT 1 QUART

MIXED BERRY SYRUP

Berries and/or berry juices
Sugar

During the preserving season, save all your odds and ends of berries and berry juices and put them in a covered container in the refrigerator. When you accumulate enough to make a respectable batch of syrup (4 or 5 cups), put them in a saucepan and bring to a boil. Reduce the heat and simmer for 5 minutes. Strain through a moistened jelly bag overnight, but don't squeeze the bag. Add ¾ cup sugar for each 2 cups juice and bring to a boil. Reduce heat to simmer and cook slowly for 5 to 10 minutes. This makes a delicious syrup with many uses. If you wish to create a heavier syrup, simply add more sugar.

SERVINGS VARY

When gathering wild berries, keep a separate container for odds and ends of berries that can all be thrown in together. Mixed berries can be used for syrups, jams, jellies, and sauces. Often you may find only a handful each of several kinds and not enough to keep separate containers for each.

WILD RASPBERRY SYRUP

3 cups wild raspberries
½ cup water
Sugar

In a saucepan, simmer the raspberries in the water for 5 minutes. Pour into a damp jelly bag and strain overnight; do not squeeze the bag. Put the pulp through a sieve and use for raspberry puree in making jam or other dishes. Pour the juice into a saucepan and stir in sugar (¼ cup sugar for each cup juice). Bring to a slow boil, then reduce heat and simmer for 10 minutes. Serve warm or at room temperature. This is an excellent sweetener for beverages and as a sauce for pancakes.

SERVINGS VARY

RED HUCKLEBERRY SYRUP

Red huckleberries
Water
Sugar
Pinch of salt

Cook berries in a small amount of water. Place the softened berries in a jelly bag and drain overnight; do not squeeze bag or syrup will be cloudy. Add 2 cups sugar to each quart of juice. Add a pinch of salt. Cook over low heat until the berry liquid becomes syrupy. It thickens as it cools. Pour into sterilized canning jars and seal or keep refrigerated. This syrup is delicious on sundaes, hotcakes, and waffles.

SERVINGS VARY

ROSE HIP SYRUP

4 cups rose hips, cleaned

2 cups water

2 cups sugar

In a saucepan, simmer the rose hips and water over low heat for 20 minutes. Strain through a jelly bag or cheesecloth to remove sediment. Return the juice to the pan and add the sugar. Boil again for 5 minutes. Store in the refrigerator, where it will keep almost indefinitely. This is especially good in combination with other juices or syrups because of its high vitamin C content. The pulp may be saved and used with other fruit for jam.

MAKES ABOUT 2 CUPS

BLUEBERRY SAUCE

½ cup sugar

2 tablespoons cornstarch

Pinch of salt

1 cup blueberry juice

1 cup water

3 tablespoons butter

2 tablespoons lemon juice

Combine the sugar, cornstarch, and salt in a saucepan and mix until smooth. Add the juice and water gradually and keep stirring. Simmer over low heat until thick and clear. Remove from heat and stir in the butter and lemon juice until combined. This sauce is wonderful on waffles or blueberry hotcakes.

MAKES ABOUT 2 CUPS

CRANBERRY BUTTER SAUCE

2 cups Whole Berry Cranberry Sauce (page 52)

¼ cup butter

¼ cup brown sugar or maple syrup

Ground cinnamon

Combine the sauce, butter, sugar or syrup, and cinnamon in a pot and heat just to the boiling point. Serve hot on waffles or pancakes.

MAKES ABOUT 2¼ CUPS

EASIEST BERRY SAUCE

1 cup berry juice

1 cup water

½ cup sugar

1 tablespoon cornstarch

In a saucepan, bring the juice and water to a simmer over medium heat. Mix the sugar and cornstarch with a small amount of the liquid, then return all to the hot juice. Cook, stirring, until the sauce is thick and clear. This sauce is excellent served on berry desserts.

MAKES ABOUT 2 CUPS

FRUIT JUICE SAUCE

1 cup sugar

1 tablespoon cornstarch

Pinch of salt

½ cup boiling water

1 cup juice of blueberries, raspberries, or strawberries

2 tablespoons lemon or orange juice

A few fresh, whole berries, optional

Mix together the sugar, cornstarch, and salt in a saucepan and slowly add the boiling water. Boil for 5 minutes and then stir in the juices. Cool and stir in a few whole berries, if desired.

MAKES ABOUT 1½ CUPS

CRANBERRY-PORT DESSERT SAUCE

1 cup sugar

½ cup Port wine

2 thin lemon slices

1 cinnamon stick

1¾ cups lowbush cranberries

In a saucepan, combine the sugar, Port, lemon slices, and cinnamon and bring to a boil. Reduce the heat and simmer for 5 minutes. Add the cranberries and cook gently, just long enough for the skins to begin popping. Remove from heat. This festive-looking sauce for holiday ice cream can be served hot or cold.

MAKES ABOUT 2 CUPS

MELBA SAUCE

2 cups salmonberries or raspberries

¼ cup wild berry jelly

Sugar

1 teaspoon cornstarch

1 tablespoon cold water

Put the berries in a saucepan and place over medium-high heat. Cook, stirring occasionally, until the berries start to fall apart. Remove from the heat. When the berries are partially cooled, press them through a strainer to remove seeds. Return the berry puree to the saucepan. Add the wild berry jelly and place back over medium-high heat, stirring until the jelly is melted. Stir in enough sugar to suit your taste. Mix the cornstarch and cold water into a smooth paste and pour into the berry mixture. Simmer and stir until the sauce thickens slightly. Strain again. This sauce is good on ice cream, puddings, and fresh fruit.

MAKES ABOUT 1½ CUPS

Alaska Natives and Eskimos often refer to cloudberries (Rubus chamaemorus) as salmonberries because of their salmon color. They are not the same berry as Rubus spectabilis, which is more commonly accepted as salmonberry over the extent of its range.

RASPBERRY SAUCE

2 cups raspberries, thawed if frozen

¼ cup sugar

2 tablespoons cornstarch

1 tablespoon lemon juice

¼ teaspoon almond extract, optional

Drain the juice from thawed raspberries and add enough water to make 1½ cups liquid. In a saucepan, combine the liquid with the sugar, cornstarch, and lemon juice. Cook, stirring, until mixture comes to a boil. Boil for 1 minute. Remove from the heat and stir in the almond extract, if desired. Serve this sauce on sundaes, angel food cake, puddings, or cream pie.

MAKES ABOUT 1½ CUPS

RASPBERRY AND WINE SAUCE

2 cups raspberries, thawed if frozen

¼ cup Port wine

2 tablespoons cornstarch

Finely grated zest and juice of 1 orange

Place the berries in a saucepan with the Port. Mix the cornstarch, orange zest, and juice; add to the berries. Place over medium heat and stir until the mixture becomes thick and transparent. Cover and refrigerate for at least 24 hours before serving.

MAKES ABOUT 1½ CUPS

VARIATION: Substitute strawberries for the raspberries.

RED HUCKLEBERRY SAUCE

Karen Holstad • Petersburg, Alaska

1 cup red huckleberries

¼ cup sugar

3 tablespoons cold water

2 tablespoons light corn syrup

1 tablespoon cornstarch

2 teaspoons lemon juice

Combine the berries, sugar, 2 tablespoons of the cold water, and the corn syrup in a saucepan. Bring to a boil. Blend the cornstarch and the remaining 1 tablespoon of cold water, stirring gradually into the berry mixture. Cook until thickened, stirring constantly. Stir in the lemon juice and remove from the heat. Let the sauce cool completely, then refrigerate until chilled. This topping is especially good on ice cream, Swedish pancakes, or waffles.

MAKES ABOUT ¾ CUP

SIMPLE SUNDAE SAUCE

2 cups wild strawberries

¾ cup sugar

Using a fork, crush the berries just enough to get their juices flowing. In a saucepan, combine the crushed berries and sugar. Let stand for 2 hours. Bring the berry mixture slowly to a boil and cook for exactly 1 minute. Allow to cool. Try this over vanilla ice cream.

MAKES ABOUT 1¼ CUPS

PIES AND TARTS

MASTER PIECRUST MIX

University of Alaska Cooperative Extension Service

7 cups all-purpose flour, sifted

4 teaspoons salt

1 pound lard (about 2 cups) or vegetable shortening (about 2½ cups)

In a bowl, mix together the flour and salt thoroughly. Cut in the lard or shortening, using a pastry blender, two knives, or fingertips, until the fat particles are no larger than small peas.

Use what you need and store the rest for a later date. If you're using lard in the recipe, store the Master Piecrust Mix in the refrigerator. If you're using shortening, store the mix in an airtight container.

MAKES ENOUGH FOR 6 SINGLE-CRUST PIE PASTRIES OR 4 DOUBLE-CRUST PIE PASTRIES

SINGLE-CRUST PIE PASTRY

University of Alaska Cooperative Extension Service

1½ cups **Master Piecrust Mix**

2 to 3 tablespoons **ice-cold water**

Little by little, sprinkle the cold water over the Master Piecrust Mix, blending with a fork, until the dough just starts to hold together. Let stand for 5 minutes. Roll out the pie dough according to your recipe.

MAKES ONE 8- OR 9-INCH PIE PASTRY

VARIATIONS:

- Double-Crust Pie Pastry: Follow the directions for the Single-Crust Pie Pastry, using 2½ cups Master Piecrust Mix and 4 to 6 tablespoons water. Makes one 8- or 9-inch double-crust pie pastry or one 10-inch single pie pastry.

- Baked Pie Pastry: Prepare the Single-Crust Pie Pastry and roll it out into a circle that's 1-inch larger than your pie pan. Transfer the pastry to the pie pan and trim the edges. Line the pastry in the pan with parchment paper and fill with pie weights. Bake until light golden brown, 10 to 12 minutes. Carefully remove the pie weights and let the crust cool completely before filling. Makes one 8- or 9-inch pie pastry.

CRUMB CRUST

1½ cups graham cracker or vanilla wafer crumbs, finely crushed

⅓ cup melted butter

2 to 3 tablespoons sugar

Preheat the oven to 350°F. In a bowl, mix together the crumbs, butter, and sugar together thoroughly. (Use 3 tablespoons sugar for the graham cracker crumbs, 2 tablespoons for the vanilla wafers.)

Spread the crumb mixture evenly over a greased 9-inch pie pan, then press into place to form a shell. A handy way to ensure an even crust is to press another 9-inch pie pan into the crumbs.

Bake the pie shell until slightly firm, about 10 minutes. Cool completely, then chill in the refrigerator until ready to fill.

MAKES ONE 9-INCH PIECRUST

BASIC WILD BERRY PIE

1 Double-Crust Pie Pastry (page 73)

1 cup sugar

¼ cup all-purpose flour

Pinch of salt

3 cups wild berries

2 tablespoons butter

¼ cup cold water

Preheat the oven to 450°F. Prepare the pastry, then divide it in half. Roll out each half on a lightly floured work surface into a 10-inch circle. Line a 9-inch pie pan with the bottom crust.

Sift together the sugar, flour, and salt and sprinkle over the berries in a bowl; toss lightly to mix. (Tart berries may require more sugar.) Pour the berry mixture into the pastry-lined pan. Dot with the butter. Pour the cold water over the ingredients in the pan. Place the top crust over the fruit, lining up the edges, and crimp the edges to seal. Prick the crust to vent steam. Bake for 10 minutes, then reduce the heat to 375°F and bake until pie appears well done, another 30 minutes.

Hint: Place a sheet of foil somewhat larger than the pie on the shelf below it to prevent a mess in the oven if the filling bubbles over.

MAKES 8 SERVINGS

BERRY CHIFFON PIE

2¼ cups fresh strawberries
or raspberries

1 cup sugar

1 envelope unflavored
gelatin

¼ cup cold water

½ cup hot water

1 tablespoon lemon juice

Pinch of salt

½ cup heavy cream

2 large egg whites

1 Crumb Crust, using
graham crackers (page 74),
baked and chilled

In a bowl, crush the berries and sprinkle with ½ cup of the sugar. Allow to stand for 30 minutes.

Soften the gelatin in cold water, then dissolve it in hot water. Allow to cool. Add the sweetened berries, lemon juice, and salt to the gelatin; chill until partly set.

Whip the cream until stiff and fold into the berry mixture. Beat the egg whites until peaks form when beater is removed. Slowly add the remaining ½ cup sugar into the egg whites and continue beating until peaks hold their form. Carefully fold the berry mixture into the sweetened egg whites. Pour the combined mixtures into the crumb crust. Chill until firm. Garnish with extra berries.

MAKES 8 SERVINGS

BLUEBERRY-LEMON PIE

1¼ cups ginger ale

1 (3-ounce) package
lemon gelatin

1 pint vanilla ice cream

1 cup blueberries

½ cup sugar

1 Baked Pie Pastry (page 73)

Slivered candied ginger,
for serving

Bring the ginger ale to a boil, then remove from heat. Dissolve the gelatin in the warm ginger ale. Immediately add the ice cream and stir until melted. Chill until the mixture holds its shape when dropped from a spoon.

In another bowl, combine the blueberries and sugar. Carefully fold the sweetened berries into the gelatin mixture. Pour the combined mixtures into the prebaked pie shell and refrigerate for several hours.

To serve, sprinkle slivered candied ginger on top.

MAKES 8 SERVINGS

BLUEBERRY PIE

Jane Helmer • Fairbanks, Alaska

2 cups blueberries
1¼ cups sugar
½ cup plus ⅔ cup water
2 tablespoons cornstarch
1 Baked Pie Pastry (page 73)
Whipped cream

Mix berries, sugar, and ½ cup water. Bring to a boil and simmer gently until the berries produce juice. Dissolve the cornstarch in ⅔ cup water. Slowly add to the hot berries and cook gently, stirring all the while, until thick. Pour the filling into the prebaked pie crust. Chill. Cover with whipped cream.

MAKES 8 SERVINGS

CLOUDBERRY PIE

Lois Armstrong • Brookings, Oregon

1 Double-Crust Pie Pastry
(page 73)
3 cups cloudberries
1 cup sugar
3 tablespoons all-purpose
flour
2 tablespoons butter

Preheat oven to 350°F. Prepare the pastry, divide in half, then roll each one out on a lightly floured work surface into a 10-inch circle. Line a pie pan with the bottom crust. Gently mix the berries, sugar, and flour—be sure not to crush the berries—and pour into pie pan. Dot with the butter. Place top crust on pie and seal edges. Bake until the crust is nicely browned, 45 to 50 minutes.

MAKES 8 SERVINGS

VARIATION: Serviceberry Pie: Substitute serviceberries for cloudberries. Add an additional ¼ cup sugar, and additional 1 tablespoon butter, and 1 tablespoon of lemon juice.

Barbara Maxwell • Rabbit Creek, Alaska

CRANBERRY CUSTARD PIE

Barbara Johnson • Anchorage, Alaska

1 Single-Crust Pie Pastry (page 73)

4 cups lowbush cranberries

1½ cups sugar

3 large eggs, well-beaten

¼ teaspoon salt

½ teaspoon ground cinnamon

1¼ cups milk

Preheat the oven to 450°F. Prepare the pastry, then roll out on a lightly floured work surface into a 10-inch circle. Line a 9-inch pie pan with the pastry.

Process the cranberries and 1¼ cups of the sugar in a food processor until finely chopped. Heat the cranberry mixture in a saucepan until the sugar is dissolved, stirring all the while. Allow to cool thoroughly, then pour into the pie shell.

In a bowl, whisk together the beaten eggs, the remaining ¼ cup sugar, salt, and cinnamon. In a saucepan, warm the milk over medium heat, watching carefully, until it just starts to come to a boil. Immediately remove the pan from the heat. Whisk about ½ cup of the warm milk into the egg mixture to warm it up. While whisking, slowly pour the remaining ¾ milk mixture into the egg mixture to form a custard. Pour the custard over the berry mixture. Bake for 10 minutes, then reduce heat to 350°F and continue baking until pie appears done, another 35 minutes.

MAKES 8 SERVINGS

CRANBERRY PIE

3 cups lowbush cranberries

1½ cups sugar

3 tablespoons water

1½ tablespoons cornstarch

1 teaspoon vanilla extract

Pinch of salt

1 Double-Crust Pie Pastry (page 73)

Preheat the oven to 450°F.

In a saucepan, combine the lowbush cranberries, sugar, water, cornstarch, vanilla, and salt and bring to a slow boil for 1 minute. Set aside to cool.

Prepare the pastry, divide in half, then roll each one out on a lightly floured work surface into a 10-inch circle. Line a pie pan with the bottom crust. Cut the remaining pastry into strips for a lattice top. Pour the cranberry mixture into the pie shell and cover with lattice pastry strips. Bake for 10 to 15 minutes, then reduce the oven heat to 350°F and continue baking until the pie appears done, another 30 minutes.

MAKES 8 SERVINGS

CRAN-RAISIN PIE

1 Double-Crust Pie Pastry (page 73)

1 cup sugar

1 tablespoon cornstarch

Pinch of salt

¼ cup boiling water

¼ teaspoon vanilla extract

¾ cup raisins

1½ cups lowbush cranberries

Milk, for glazing

Preheat the oven to 425°F. Prepare the pastry, divide in half, then roll each one out on a lightly floured work surface into a 10-inch circle. Line a pie pan with the bottom crust.

In a bowl, mix together the sugar, cornstarch, and salt. Add the water, vanilla, and raisins. Beat until smooth. Add the cranberries; stir until well mixed. Pour the cranberry mixture into the pie shell. Cover with the top crust, lining up the edges. Flute the pie edges and prick the crust to allow steam to escape. Brush the top crust with milk, if desired, for a shiny, golden finish. Bake for 10 minutes, then reduce heat to 350°F and continue baking until the pie appears done, another 35 minutes.

MAKES 8 SERVINGS

CREAM-AND-SUGAR BERRY PIE

Virginia Culver • Chugiak, Alaska

1 Single Crust Pie Pastry (page 73)

4 cups fresh berries

1 cup heavy cream

⅔ cup sugar

4 teaspoons all-purpose flour

¼ teaspoon salt

Preheat the oven to 350°F. Prepare the pastry, then roll it out on a lightly floured work surface into a 10-inch circle. Line a 9-inch pie pan with the crust.

Pour the berries into the pie shell. In a bowl, mix together the cream, sugar, flour, and salt and pour over the berries. Bake until the crust becomes brown and the filling is set, about 45 minutes. Serve while still warm.

MAKES 8 SERVINGS

CROWBERRY PIE

1 Baked Pie Pastry (page 73)

4 cups fresh or frozen crowberries

1 cup sugar

¼ cup water

3 tablespoons cornstarch

1 tablespoon lemon juice

Pinch of salt

1 tablespoon butter

Whipped cream, for serving

Pour 2 cups of the berries into the prebaked pie shell, spreading them evenly. Put the remaining 2 cups berries in a saucepan along with the sugar, water, cornstarch, lemon juice, and salt. Cook over medium-low heat, stirring occasionally, until fairly thick, 5 to 10 minutes. Stir in the butter and set aside to cool slightly. Pour the cooked berry mixture over the raw berries in the pie shell. Chill for 3 or 4 hours in the refrigerator and serve with whipped cream or other topping.

MAKES 8 SERVINGS

VARIATION: Substitute 2 cups blueberries or 2 cups lowbush cranberries for half the crowberries. Add more sugar when substituting cranberries.

DOUBLE-GOOD BLUEBERRY PIE

Mrs. Ross Bradford • Creswell, Oregon

1 cup sugar

3 tablespoons cornstarch

⅛ teaspoon salt

½ cup water

4 cups blueberries

1 tablespoon butter

1 tablespoon lemon juice

1 Baked Pie Pastry (page 73)

Whipped cream, for serving

In a saucepan, combine the sugar, cornstarch, and salt. Add the water and 2 cups of the blueberries. Cook over medium-high heat until the mixture boils and is thick and clear, stirring all the while. Remove from heat and stir in the butter and lemon juice. Let cool.

Mix the remaining 2 cups uncooked blueberries into the cooled berry mixture and pour into the prebaked pie shell. Chill well. Serve with whipped cream.

MAKES 8 SERVINGS

GLAZED STRAWBERRY PIE

Florence Thornton • Anchorage, Alaska

1 Baked Pie Pastry (page 73)
1 quart strawberries
1¼ cups sugar
½ cup water
½ teaspoon cream of tartar
2 large egg whites
Pinch of salt
½ teaspoon vanilla extract

Pour the berries into the baked pie shell, spreading them out evenly.

Mix the sugar, water, and cream of tartar in a saucepan; cover and bring to a boil. Uncover and continue cooking until the syrup "spins a thread." (Spoon up some syrup and slowly begin to pour it back into the pan from a height of about 18 inches. If threadlike wisps flow from the spoon, the syrup is ready.) Put the egg whites in a clean bowl, add the salt, and beat until stiff. While continuing to beat, gradually pour the syrup into the egg whites. Continue beating until the syrup and egg white mixture forms stiff peaks. Stir in the vanilla.

Pile the egg white on top of berries in the pie shell, leaving an uncovered center area. Allow to cool before serving, but do not refrigerate.

Note: This recipe contains uncooked eggs, which may increase your risk for foodborne illness.

MAKES 8 SERVINGS

KUCHEN

Mrs. Ed Seyfert • Unalakleet, Alaska

1 Single-Crust Pie Pastry (page 73)

4 tablespoons all-purpose flour

1½ cups, plus 1 tablespoon sugar

2 cups berries of your choice

3 large eggs

1½ teaspoon salt

1⅓ cups evaporated milk

1⅓ cups water

Preheat oven to 425°F. Prepare the pastry, then roll out on a lightly floured work surface into a 10-inch circle. Line a 9-inch pie pan with the pastry.

Sprinkle 1 tablespoon of the flour and 1 tablespoon of the sugar over the crust to prevent it from becoming soggy. Sprinkle the berries over the sugar-flour mixture.

To prepare the custard, beat the eggs with the remaining 1½ cups sugar, the remaining 3 tablespoons flour, and the salt, using a wooden spoon. (Do not use a mixer.) In another bowl, dilute the milk with the water; stir into the egg mixture. Pour this custard over the berries. Bake for 20 minutes, then reduce the heat to 400°F and continue baking until custard is set, 25 minutes. Almost any berry or other fruit will work well in this kuchen.

MAKES 8 SERVINGS

NAGOONBERRY PIE

Maxcine Williams • Eugene, Oregon

3 large egg yolks, beaten

1 cup sugar

1 cup nagoonberry juice

Pinch of salt

1 envelope unflavored gelatin

½ teaspoon cream of tartar

3 large egg whites

1 Baked Pie Pastry (page 73)

Whipped cream, for serving

In the top part of a double boiler, mix the egg yolks, ½ cup of the sugar, ½ cup of the berry juice, and the salt. Place over the lower part of the double boiler filled with simmering water and cook until the mixture thickens, 10 to 12 minutes, stirring gently as it cooks.

Soften the gelatin in the remaining ½ cup juice. Remove the egg mixture from the heat and stir in the gelatin mixture. Let cool, then refrigerate until chilled.

Mix together the remaining ½ cup sugar and the cream of tartar. In a clean bowl, beat the egg whites until foamy, then gradually beat in the sugar mixture. Continue beating until stiff peaks form.

Fold together the egg white mixture and the egg yolk mixture, then pour into prebaked pie shell and put back in the refrigerator to chill. When ready to serve, top with whipped cream.

Note: This recipe contains uncooked eggs, which may increase your risk for foodborne illness.

MAKES 8 SERVINGS

In the early 1970s, nagoonberries were sold by an Alaska preserve company for about $45 a pint!

POP-IN-A-PAN PIE

FOR THE MAKE-AHEAD FILLING

4 quarts fresh blueberries

3½ cups sugar

¾ cup quick-cooking tapioca

6 tablespoons lemon juice

1 teaspoon salt

1 Double-Crust Pie Pastry (page 73) for each pie

1 tablespoon butter for each pie

This recipe makes enough filling for four 9-inch pies; the filling can be stored for up to 6 months before use.

To make the filling, wash and drain the berries, then mix well with the sugar, tapioca, lemon juice, and salt. Line four 9-inch pie pans with heavy-duty foil, allowing the foil to extend 5 inches beyond the rim of each pan. Pour the filling equally into the foil-lined pans. Fold the foil loosely over the tops and freeze until solid. Remove the frozen filling from the pans, wrap tightly with foil, and return to the freezer.

To bake each pie, preheat the oven to 425°F. Prepare the pastry, divide in half, then roll each one out on a lightly floured work surface into a 10-inch circle. Line a pie pan with the bottom crust. Take one portion of frozen filling from freezer and remove the foil; do not let the filling thaw. Pop the frozen filling into the pie pan and dot with butter. Add the top crust, lining up the edges, seal the edges, and cut slits in the top crust for vents. Bake until the filling boils up with heavy bubbles that do not burst and the top crust is golden brown, 45 to 60 minutes. Serve warm.

MAKES FOUR 9-INCH PIES

RASPBERRY FLUFF PIE

1 tablespoon unflavored gelatin

½ cup cold water

½ cup sugar

1½ cups crushed raspberries

1 tablespoon lemon juice

1 large egg white

½ cup evaporated milk, chilled

⅓ cup cream cheese, softened

1 Crumb Crust (page 74, using vanilla wafers), baked and chilled

In the top part of a double boiler, mix the gelatin and ¼ cup of the cold water and let stand for 5 minutes. Add the sugar and remaining ¼ cup cold water and mix well. Place over the bottom part of the double boiler over simmering water and cook, stirring, until the gelatin and sugar dissolve, then remove it from heat. Add the crushed berries and lemon juice. Mix well, then chill, stirring occasionally, until the mixture starts to thicken.

In a clean bowl, beat the egg white until stiff peaks form. Carefully fold the egg white into the chilled berry mixture. Beat together the evaporated milk and cream cheese together for 2 minutes, then fold into the berry mixture. Pour into the prebaked pie shell and chill for at least 3 hours before serving.

MAKES 8 SERVINGS

ROSE HIP CRUMBLE PIE

1 Single-Crust Pie Pastry
(page 73)

1 cup dried rose hips

¼ cup milk

1½ cups all-purpose flour

2 teaspoons baking powder

Pinch of salt

1¾ cups brown sugar

½ cup vegetable shortening

2 large egg yolks, beaten

2 large egg whites

Pecan halves, optional

Preheat oven to 350°F. Prepare the pastry, then roll out on a lightly floured work surface into a 10-inch circle. Line a 9-inch pie pan with the pastry.

Mix the rose hips with the milk and set aside to soften. In a bowl, sift together the flour, baking powder, and salt. In another bowl, cream the brown sugar and shortening. Add the flour mixture and mix until crumbly. Set aside 1 cup of the mixture for the topping. Add the egg yolks and the milk and rose hips mixture to the remaining crumbly mixture. In another bowl, beat the egg whites until they form stiff peaks. Fold into the rose hips mixture. Spoon into the pie pan and sprinkle the crumbly topping evenly over the top. If desired, garnish with pecan halves. Bake until pie appears well done, 35 to 45 minutes.

MAKES 8 SERVINGS

ROSE HIP PIE

1 Double-Crust Pie Pastry
(page 73)

1½ cups rose hips (best if
not quite ripe)

1 cup sugar

1½ tablespoons cornstarch

½ cup butter, melted

2 large eggs, beaten

1 cup light corn syrup

1 teaspoon vanilla extract

Dash of fresh lemon juice

Pinch of salt

Preheat the oven to 350°F. Prepare the pastry, divide it in half, then roll each one out on a lightly floured work surface into a 10-inch circle. Line a 9-inch pie pan with the bottom crust. Cut the remaining pastry into strips for a lattice top.

Clean and seed the rose hips. Mix the sugar and cornstarch, then blend in the melted butter. Add the eggs, corn syrup, vanilla, lemon juice, and salt; mix. Stir in the rose hips. Pour into the pie shell and cover with lattice pastry strips. Bake until the pastry is nicely browned, 45 minutes.

MAKES 8 SERVINGS

It is a good idea to pick a few rose hips with each container of berries, no matter what kind. When you process the berries, the rose hips can be cleaned and processed with them for an extra dose of vitamins.

SALMONBERRY CREAM PIE

6 cups salmonberries, plus a few extra for garnish

⅔ cup sugar

3 tablespoons cornstarch

Pinch of salt

1 baked 10-inch pie shell

Whipped cream

Crush 2 cups of the berries and force them through a sieve. Add enough water to the berry puree to equal 1½ cups and pour into a saucepan. In a bowl, mix together the sugar, cornstarch, and salt and add to the berry mixture. Cook over medium-high heat, stirring constantly, until the mixture is well thickened, about 5 minutes. Allow to cool.

Place the remaining 4 cups berries in the prebaked pie shell, then pour the cooled cooked berry mixture over the top. Spread the whipped cream over the top of the pie. Garnish with a few perfect, whole salmonberries.

MAKES 8 SERVINGS

STRAWBERRY PIES

Hannah Weber • Quincy, Washington

½ pint heavy cream

1 heaping cup strawberries

¾ cup sugar

2 tablespoons lemon juice

2 large egg whites

¼ teaspoon salt

2 Baked Pie Pastries (page 73)

Whip the cream and refrigerate. In a bowl, beat together the strawberries, sugar, lemon juice, egg whites, and salt until smooth, about 5 minutes. Fold in the whipped cream and divide the mixture among the prebaked pie shells. Refrigerate for 6 hours. This recipe works well with other berries, too.

MAKES 16 SERVINGS

YUKON CHERRY PIE

1 Double-Crust Pie Pastry
(page 73)

1½ cups lowbush
cranberries

1 cup sugar

1 cup water

1 teaspoon vanilla extract

¼ teaspoon salt

4 to 5 tablespoons
all-purpose flour

1 large egg, slightly beaten

Preheat the oven to 350°F. Prepare the pastry, divide it in half, then roll each one out on a lightly floured work surface into a 10-inch circle. Line a pie pan with the bottom crust.

Cook the berries, sugar, water, vanilla, and salt until the berries are soft. Thicken the berry mixture with a paste made from the flour and a little bit of cold water. Allow the berry mixture to cool, then blend in the slightly beaten egg.

Pour the berry mixture into the crust. Cover with the top crust, lining up the edges, and bake until crust is well browned, 45 minutes. This is a good substitute for cherry pie.

MAKES 8 SERVINGS

WILD STRAWBERRY PIE

Mary Taylor • Moose Pass, Alaska

1 quart strawberries

1 Baked Pie Pastry (page 73)

1 cup sugar

3 tablespoons cornstarch

Whipped cream, for serving

Place half of the raw berries in the prebaked pie shell. In a saucepan, crush the remaining berries. Mix the sugar with the cornstarch and mix with the crushed berries. Cook over medium-high heat, stirring, until the mixture is clear and thick, 5 to 10 minutes. Let cool.

Pour the cooled berry mixture over the raw berries in the pie shell. Serve with whipped cream.

MAKES 8 SERVINGS

BERRY MERINGUE "TARTS"

4 large egg whites

1 teaspoon vanilla extract

½ teaspoon white wine vinegar

Pinch of salt

1 cup sugar

½ cup quick-cooking oats

4 cups whipped cream

2 cups salmonberries, raspberries, strawberries, or cloudberries

Preheat the oven to 275°F.

In a clean bowl, beat the egg whites, gradually adding the vanilla, vinegar, and salt. Continue beating until frothy. Gradually add the sugar, beating well after each addition. Continue to beat until the mixture forms stiff peaks. Gently fold in the oats.

Line a baking sheet with parchment paper. Make 7 or 8 equal mounds of the egg white batter on the baking sheet. Using a spoon, form hollows in the centers of the mounds and shape their sides to resemble tart shells. Bake until dry and crisp, 45 to 60 minutes. Allow to cool for 1 hour or more.

To serve, combine the whipped cream with the berries and spoon into the tartlike shells.

MAKES 7 OR 8 SERVINGS

BLUEBERRY POCKETS

University of Alaska Cooperative Extension Service

Butter, for greasing

1 cup fresh blueberries

3 tablespoons sugar

1¾ cups all-purpose flour

2½ teaspoons baking powder

¾ teaspoon salt

½ teaspoon ground cinnamon

⅛ teaspoon ground allspice

⅓ cup vegetable shortening

1 cup shredded wheat cereal, crushed to crumbs

1½ teaspoons finely grated lemon zest or dried lemon peel granules

⅔ cup milk

Heavy cream, for serving

Preheat oven to 450°F. Butter a 12-cup muffin pan.

In a bowl, mix together the berries and 2 tablespoons of the sugar and let stand to release the juices. Sift together the flour, the remaining 1 tablespoon sugar, baking powder, salt, cinnamon, and allspice. Mix in the shortening until crumbly. Stir in the cereal crumbs and lemon zest. Add the milk and stir until the mixture holds together.

Knead the mixture lightly 10 times on a floured board. Using a rolling pin, roll out the dough to a ¼-inch-thick rectangle. Cut the dough into twelve 3-inch squares and place one square in each cup in the prepared muffin pan. Fill each cup with a heaping tablespoon of the berry mixture. Bring the corners of dough together and press the edges together firmly. Bake until brown and bubbly, about 20 minutes. Serve warm with cream poured over the top.

MAKES 12 SERVINGS

VARIATION: To form tart shells, roll out the pastry and cut it into 3-inch circles. Press the circles over an inverted muffin pan to shape. Remove the pastry carefully, set the muffin tins upright, and set the pastry inside. Now you're ready to drop in the filling and bake!

FRENCH STRAWBERRY CREAM TART

TART SHELL
1½ cups all-purpose flour

½ teaspoon baking powder

Pinch of salt

½ cup butter

1 large egg, slightly beaten

½ cup sugar

FILLING
⅔ cup sugar

4 tablespoons cornstarch

Pinch of salt

2 cups milk

2 large eggs

½ teaspoon vanilla extract

½ teaspoon lemon extract

2 cups strawberries

Preheat the oven to 425°F. To make the tart shell, sift together the flour, baking powder, and salt. Blend in the butter until the mixture attains a mealy texture. Add the sugar to one slightly beaten egg and blend; stir into the flour mixture and mix well. Press the dough into the bottom and sides of a greased 9-inch pie pan. Bake partially for about 20 minutes, then allow to cool.

To make the filling, combine the sugar, cornstarch, and salt in the top of a double boiler. Gradually stir in the milk and place over the bottom part of the double boiler over low heat and cook, stirring constantly until the mixture is thick and smooth. In a heatproof bowl, whisk together the eggs. While whisking, pour about ½ cup of the hot mixture over the eggs to warm them slightly, then gradually whisk in the remaining hot mixture. Return the mixture to the double boiler and cook over boiling water for 5 minutes more, stirring all the while. Allow to cool, then stir in the vanilla and lemon extract. Pour the mixture into the tart shell. Let cool.

Chill in the refrigerator until ready to serve. Just before serving, arrange the strawberries over the top of the custard.

MAKES 8 SERVINGS

COBBLERS AND FRIENDS

WILD BERRY COBBLER

FILLING

½ to 1½ cups sugar
(amount varies with
tartness of berries)

1 tablespoon cornstarch

1 cup boiling water

3 cups your choice of berries

1 tablespoon butter

Your choice of spices,
optional

TOPPING

1 cup all-purpose flour

1 tablespoon sugar

1½ teaspoons baking
powder

½ teaspoon salt

¼ cup vegetable shortening

½ cup milk

Preheat the oven to 400°F. Butter a 10-by-6-inch baking pan.

To prepare the filling, combine the sugar and cornstarch and blend in boiling water. Stir over medium heat until the mixture has boiled for 1 minute. Add the berries, then pour into the prepared pan. Dot with butter and sprinkle on spices if you wish. Keep the berries warm in the oven while the topping is being prepared.

To prepare the topping, sift together the flour, sugar, baking powder, and salt. Work in the shortening, then stir in the milk until a soft dough is formed. Drop spoonfuls over the hot berry mixture and bake until the filling is bubbling and the topping is golden brown, about 30 minutes. Serve warm.

MAKES 8 TO 10 SERVINGS

SIMPLE BERRY COBBLER

Eleanor Prince • Wrangell, Alaska

¼ cup butter

1 cup all-purpose flour

1 cup sugar

¾ cup milk

2 cups your choice of berries

Whipped cream or ice cream, for serving, optional

Preheat the oven to 350°F. Melt the butter in a 1½-quart casserole dish. Mix together the flour, sugar, and milk, then pour over the melted butter in the dish. Do not stir. Sprinkle the berries over the flour-milk mixture, spreading them evenly. Bake until the filling is bubbling and the topping is golden brown, about 30 minutes. Serve warm or cold, topped with whipped cream or ice cream, if desired.

MAKES 8 TO 10 SERVINGS

CRANBERRY COBBLER

Lucile Crocker • Elk City, Idaho

Butter, for greasing

1⅔ cups sugar

⅓ cup plus ¾ cup purchased dry pancake mix

1 teaspoon finely grated lemon zest

4 cups lowbush cranberries

1 large egg, beaten

¼ cup melted butter

Heavy cream or ice cream, for serving

Preheat the oven to 375°F. Butter a 9-inch square baking pan.

In a bowl, mix together 1 cup of the sugar, ⅓ cup of the pancake mix, and the lemon zest. Add the berries and toss lightly. Pour into the prepared pan. In a bowl, combine the remaining ¾ cup pancake mix and ⅔ cup sugar. Stir in the beaten egg until the mixture resembles coarse crumbs. Sprinkle this mixture evenly over the cranberry mixture in the pan. Sprinkle with the melted butter and bake until the filling is bubbling and the topping is golden brown, about 35 to 40 minutes. Serve with cream or ice cream.

MAKES 8 TO 10 SERVINGS

JUICY HUCKLEBERRY COBBLER

Lillian Wisniewski • Depoe Bay, Oregon

3 tablespoons butter, plus more for greasing

2½ cups sugar

1 cup all-purpose flour

1 teaspoon baking powder

½ teaspoon salt

½ cup milk

1 quart fresh huckleberries or blueberries

1½ cups boiling water

Ice cream, for serving

Preheat the oven to 375°F. Generously butter a large baking dish.

Cream ½ cup of the sugar and 1 tablespoon of the butter together. Sift together the flour, baking powder, and salt. Add the flour mixture to the sugar mixture and mix well. Gradually stir in the milk. Spread into the prepared dish. Cover the batter with the berries and dot with the remaining 2 tablespoons butter. Sprinkle with the remaining 2 cups sugar, then pour the boiling water over the top. Bake until the filling is bubbling and the topping is golden brown, about 1 hour. Serve with ice cream.

MAKES 8 TO 10 SERVINGS

Blueberries, huckleberries, and bilberries are all closely related and belong to the family of heaths.

BLUEBERRY BUCKLE

Butter, for greasing

2 cups all-purpose flour

2 teaspoons baking powder

½ teaspoon salt

1 cup sugar

¼ cup butter

1 large egg, slightly beaten

½ cup milk

2 cups blueberries

Cream

½ to ¾ cup graham cracker crumbs

Heavy cream, for serving

Preheat the oven to 375°F. Butter a 9-inch square baking pan.

In a bowl, mix together the flour, baking powder, and salt. In another bowl, cream together the sugar and butter until light and fluffy. Add the egg and beat well. Add the flour mixture, alternating with the milk, and beat until smooth. Fold in the berries and pour into the prepared pan. Sprinkle with the graham cracker crumbs. Bake until the filling is bubbling and the topping is golden brown, about 30 to 35 minutes or until done. Serve while still warm. Cut in squares and top with cream.

MAKES 8 TO 10 SERVINGS

BLUEBERRY PANDOWDY

4 cups blueberries

1 cup sugar

2 tablespoons lemon juice

1 (15-ounce) package yellow cake mix, plus ingredients listed on the package

Heavy cream, for serving

Preheat the oven to 375°F. Combine the blueberries, sugar, and lemon juice and spread into a 9-by-9-inch pan. Prepare the cake batter according to package directions. Spread the batter over the blueberry mixture in the pan. Bake until the fruit is bubbling and a toothpick inserted into the cake layer comes out clean, 20 to 25 minutes. Cut in squares and serve warm with cream.

MAKES 8 TO 10 SERVINGS

BLUEBERRY SLUMP

Karen Clark • Cassiar, British Columbia

4 cups blueberries

1¾ cups sugar

4 tablespoons cornstarch

1 teaspoon ground nutmeg

½ teaspoon ground cinnamon

3 tablespoons vegetable shortening

½ cup milk

1½ cups all-purpose flour

1½ teaspoons baking powder

¼ teaspoon salt

Cream, for serving

In a saucepan, combine the berries, 1½ cups of the sugar, cornstarch, nutmeg, and cinnamon and slowly bring the mixture to a boil over medium heat.

While the berry mixture is heating, make the dumpling batter: In a bowl, cream the shortening with the remaining ¼ cup sugar, then add the milk and blend thoroughly. In another bowl, mix together the flour, baking powder, and salt and stir into the shortening mixture. Drop the batter by spoonfuls over the boiling blueberry mixture. Cover and cook until the dumplings are light and fluffy, about 10 minutes. Serve hot with cream poured over the top.

MAKES 4 TO 6 SERVINGS

PUDDINGS AND CUSTARDS

ALASKAN FLAN

2 tablespoons sugar

3 whole large eggs, beaten

3 large egg whites, beaten

1 (13-ounce) can evaporated milk

1 (14-ounce) can sweetened condensed milk

2 tablespoons vanilla extract

2 cups sweetened crushed salmonberries or cloudberries

Preheat the oven to 350°F.

In a saucepan over medium heat, cook the sugar, stirring constantly until it turns into a dark caramel substance. Pour into a shallow baking dish. Blend together the beaten whole eggs, egg whites, and milks. Add the vanilla, then pour into the baking pan with the caramel and cover. Place the covered dish into a shallow baking pan half-filled with hot water. Bake until gently set, about 2 hours.

Remove the dish from the baking pan and set on a wire rack to cool completely. Refrigerate until well chilled.

Serve cold, with crushed berries poured over.

MAKES 6 TO 8 SERVINGS

RASPBERRY TAPIOCA PUDDING

3 cups water

½ cup currant or cranberry juice

¼ cup quick-cooking tapioca

2 cups fresh or frozen raspberries

Sugar

Pinch of salt

In a saucepan, combine the water, juice, and tapioca and boil until the tapioca is transparent, about 1 minute. Stir in the berries and sugar and salt to taste. Chill in the refrigerator and serve cold.

MAKES 4 TO 6 SERVINGS

BLUEBERRIES WITH COGNAC CUSTARD

1 cup milk

3 large egg yolks,
slightly beaten

4 tablespoons sugar

Pinch of salt

½ teaspoon vanilla extract

2 to 4 tablespoons cognac or
similar spirits

Blueberries

In a saucepan, warm the milk over medium heat, watching carefully, until it just starts to come to a boil. Immediately remove the pan from the heat.

Place the slightly beaten egg yolks in the top of a double boiler and add the sugar and salt. Place over the bottom part of the double boiler over simmering (not boiling) water. Gradually add the warm milk, slowly stirring with a wooden spoon. Continue stirring until the mixture forms a coating on the spoon. Immediately remove the custard from the heat and pour into a cool bowl. Stir in the vanilla and enough cognac to suit your taste. Pour blueberries into individual bowls and cover with the custard.

MAKES 4 SERVINGS

CROWBERRY FLUMMERY

Virginia Culver • Chugiak, Alaska

1 quart crowberries

1¼ cups sugar

½ cup hot water

1 teaspoon lemon juice

Pinch of salt

2 tablespoons cornstarch

3 tablespoons cold water

Heavy cream or ice cream, for serving

In a saucepan, mix the crowberries with the sugar, hot water, lemon juice, and salt and bring to a boil. Reduce the heat and continue cooking slowly until a thin syrup forms. Make a smooth paste of the cornstarch and cold water and stir into the crowberry mixture. Continue cooking, stirring, until the mixture is slightly thick. Allow to cool. Serve with cream or over ice cream.

MAKES 4 SERVINGS

DANISH-STYLE BERRIES

Anna Marie Davis • Anchorage, Alaska

4 cups your choice of berries

2 cups water

Sugar

½ teaspoon vanilla extract

2 tablespoons cornstarch

Finely chopped almonds

In a saucepan, combine 2 cups of the berries and the water and bring to a boil over medium-high heat. Continue boiling gently until the berries break down and the mixture is very juicy. Force the mixture through a strainer and stir in sugar to taste. Return to the saucepan; add the remaining 2 cups berries and cook until the berries are tender. Add the vanilla. Make a thickening agent by pouring a little of the hot juice into the cornstarch in a small bowl. Stir the cornstarch mixture into the boiling mixture. Add the finely chopped almonds and continue cooking, stirring, until thick. Remove from the heat and sprinkle a little sugar on top to keep a crust from forming.

MAKES 4 SERVINGS

HUCKLEBERRY STEAMED PUDDING

Alaska Wild Berry Trails

⅓ cup butter

⅔ cup sugar

2 large eggs, well-beaten

2¼ cups all-purpose flour

1 teaspoon baking powder

Pinch of salt

⅓ cup milk

Red huckleberries, ripe but firm

Prepared lemon curd, for serving

In a bowl, cream the butter, then stir in the sugar gradually. Mix in the eggs. Sift together the flour, baking powder, and salt. Add the flour mixture, alternating with the milk, to the butter-sugar mixture. Gently stir in the red huckleberries. Pour the mixture into cleaned 1-pound coffee cans until each is half full. Cover with the lids.

Place the cans on a rack in a large, wide pot of boiling water or in a steamer. Steam for 3 hours in boiling water. (Add water from time to time as it boils away.) Preheat the oven to 350°F. Remove the cans from the kettle and set them in cold water for 5 to 10 seconds. Turn the cans upside down on a baking sheet. Place the sheet in the oven for 10 minutes. Carefully turn the puddings out from the cans. Slice and serve with lemon curd.

MAKES 4 TO 6 SERVINGS

VARIATION: Instead of red huckleberries, use blueberries or lowbush cranberries.

Berries do not always ripen the same place every year so keep searching for that extra good patch. They don't always ripen at the same time either because of the variations in seasons.

STEAMED CRANBERRY PUDDING

2 cups lowbush cranberries

1⅓ cups all-purpose flour

2 teaspoons baking soda

½ teaspoon salt

¼ teaspoon ground cinnamon

¼ teaspoon ground mace

¼ teaspoon ground cloves

⅓ cup hot water

½ cup molasses

Prepared hard sauce, for serving

In a bowl, stir together the cranberries, flour, baking soda, salt, cinnamon, mace, and cloves. In another bowl, mix together the hot water and molasses and blend into the cranberry mixture. Place into well-greased pudding molds, cover, and steam for 2½ hours, making sure the water level outside the mold remains at all times at least halfway up the side of the mold. (Individual molds should be steamed for only 1 hour.)

Unmold the puddings, slice, and serve with hard sauce.

MAKES 4 SERVINGS

STEAMED RASPBERRY MUSH

2 cups all-purpose flour

1 tablespoon baking powder

1 teaspoon salt

1 tablespoon butter

¾ cup milk

4 cups raspberries

2 cups sugar

1 tablespoon lemon juice

Heavy cream, for serving

In a bowl, sift together the flour, baking powder, and salt, then work in the butter. Add the milk and mix well. In another bowl, combine the berries, sugar, and lemon juice and blend into the flour mixture. Pour into a well-buttered pudding mold, cover tightly, and steam for 45 minutes, making sure the water level remains at all times at least halfway up the sides of the mold.

Unmold, slice, and serve with cream.

MAKES 6 TO 8 SERVINGS

BAKED BLUEBERRY TAPIOCA PUDDING

½ cup pearl tapioca

6 cups cold water

3 cups blueberries

Finely grated zest and juice of 1 lemon

1 cup sugar

2 tablespoons butter

1 tablespoon ground cinnamon

1 teaspoon ground nutmeg

Liberal pinch of salt

Heavy cream, for serving

Soak the tapioca in 3 cups of water for 12 hours.

Preheat the oven to 350°F.

Drain and rinse the tapioca. In a saucepan, combine 3 cups fresh water and the tapioca and bring slowly to a boil, then simmer until tapioca is transparent, about 20 minutes, depending on the tapioca you use. As the tapioca simmers, gently mix together in a bowl the berries, lemon juice and zest, sugar, butter, cinnamon, nutmeg, and salt. Fold the berry mixture into the transparent tapioca and cook for 5 minutes. Pour into a greased baking dish and bake until the tapioca is lightly browned, about 45 minutes. Serve with cream, warm or cold.

MAKES 4 TO 6 SERVINGS

VARIATION: Old-Fashioned Cranberry Tapioca: Use 2 cups fresh or frozen lowbush cranberries and 1 tart apple, peeled and chopped, in the place of blueberries. Use only ½ teaspoon cinnamon and ½ teaspoon nutmeg. Replace the lemon zest with ¼ cup orange juice.

CAKES, CUPCAKES, AND FROSTINGS

BLUEBERRY LOAF CAKE

Vegetable shortening,
for greasing

2 large eggs, separated

1 cup sugar

½ cup vegetable shortening

1 teaspoon vanilla extract

¼ teaspoon salt

1½ cups all-purpose flour

1 teaspoon baking powder

½ teaspoon ground nutmeg

⅓ cup milk

1½ cups fresh or frozen
blueberries

Prepared lemon curd or
whipped cream, for serving

Preheat the oven to 400°F and grease a 5-by-9-inch loaf pan.

In a clean bowl, beat the egg whites until firm. Add ¼ cup of the sugar and continue beating until stiff peaks form. Set aside.

In another bowl, cream the shortening; gradually add the remaining ¾ cup sugar, vanilla, and salt. Sift together the flour, baking powder, and nutmeg and add to the shortening mixture, alternating with the milk. Carefully fold in the beaten egg whites. Gently fold in the berries. Pour into the prepared pan and bake until a toothpick or skewer inserted into the center of the cake comes out clean, about 30 minutes. Serve with lemon curd, whipped cream, or other topping.

MAKES 1 LOAF

VARIATION: For a slight caramel flavor, substitute half the white sugar with brown.

BLUEBERRY CHEESECAKE

Pacific Northwest Blueberry Growers Association

12 graham crackers, crushed

1½ cup sugar

¼ cup butter, melted

2 large eggs, well-beaten

8 ounces cream cheese

½ teaspoon vanilla extract

1 quart firm, fresh blueberries

½ cup cold water

2 tablespoons cornstarch

½ teaspoon salt

½ teaspoon lemon juice

This recipe should be prepared the night before serving.

Preheat the oven to 375°F. Mix together the crushed graham crackers, ½ cup of the sugar, and the melted butter and press into a 9-by-9-inch baking pan with removable sides. Beat together the eggs, cream cheese, another ½ cup of the sugar, and vanilla until creamy. Pour over the crushed-cracker crust and bake for 20 minutes.

In a saucepan, crush 1 cup of the berries; add the cold water, remaining ½ cup sugar, cornstarch, and salt. Cook over medium heat, stirring, until thickened. Add the lemon juice and remaining berries and heat until barely boiling. Let cool.

When the cheesecake is done, let cool on a wire rack until room temperature. Pour the berry topping over the cheesecake and refrigerate overnight. Remove the pan sides before cutting.

MAKES 8 SERVINGS

BLUEBERRY SPONGE CAKE

Mrs. William T. Foran • Seattle, Washington

Nonstick baking spray
6 large egg yolks
1 cup sugar
½ cup boiling water
1 teaspoon lemon extract
1½ cups all-purpose flour
2 teaspoons baking powder
½ teaspoon salt
4 cups crushed blueberries
½ pint whipped cream

Preheat the oven to 325°F. Spray two 9-inch round cake pans with baking spray.

In a bowl, beat the egg yolks until they are light in color. Gradually add the sugar and hot water, beating all the while. Stir in the lemon extract. Sift together the flour, baking powder, and salt and add to first mixture. Beat well. Pour the batter in the prepared pans and bake until a toothpick or skewer inserted into the center of the cakes comes out clean, about 45 minutes. Remove from the oven and allow to cool.

Remove the cakes from the pans. Mix the blueberries and whipped cream (sweetened if desired) and spread the mixture between the cake layers.

MAKES 8 SERVINGS

BLUEBERRY UPSIDE-DOWN CAKE

Virginia Culver • Chugiak, Alaska

1⅛ cups cake flour

¾ cup sugar

1½ teaspoons baking powder

½ teaspoon salt

1 large egg

¼ cup vegetable shortening, room temperature

½ teaspoon vanilla extract

3 tablespoons butter

⅔ cup packed brown sugar

1 cup firm blueberries

Whipped cream, for serving

Preheat the oven to 350°F.

In a bowl, sift together the flour, sugar, baking powder, and salt. In another bowl, beat together the egg, shortening, and vanilla. Add the flour mixture to the shortening mixture and mix well. Melt the butter in a 9-inch heavy, oven-proof skillet; sprinkle with the brown sugar and cover with a layer of blueberries. Pour the batter over this mixture and bake in the oven until a toothpick or skewer inserted into the center of the cake comes out clean, about 45 minutes. Let cool slightly on a wire rack.

Carefully invert the pan onto a serving dish. Serve with whipped cream. Works well with other wild berries too.

MAKES 8 SERVINGS

There are several tests for "doneness" in baking. Cakelike substances will spring back at once if touched lightly with the fingertip. A toothpick, skewer, or thin-bladed knife inserted into the crumb should come out clean with no dough adhering. Usually, but not always, a nicely browned crust is an indication that the dough is cooked to a turn. Cranberry bread, for instance, may still be doughy inside when the crust is really well browned, so be careful to test it.

CRANBERRY CAKE

1 cup vegetable shortening, plus more for greasing

1½ cups sugar

4 large eggs

3 cups all-purpose flour

2½ teaspoons baking powder

Pinch of salt

¾ cup milk

¼ cup orange juice

2 cups lowbush cranberries

1 cup chopped dates

½ cup chopped walnuts

2 tablespoons finely grated orange zest

1 teaspoon chopped, crystallized ginger

Cranberry Cheese Frosting (page 128)

Preheat the oven to 350°F. Grease and flour a 10-inch tube pan.

In a bowl, cream the shortening with the sugar. Add the eggs, one at a time, beating well after each addition. In another bowl, sift together the flour, baking powder, and salt. In a smaller bowl, combine the milk and orange juice, then add it to the shortening mixture, alternating with the dry ingredients. Fold in the berries, dates, nuts, orange zest, and ginger. Pour the batter into the prepared pan and bake until well browned and springy to the touch, about 1 hour, 20 minutes. When the cake is almost cool, top with the frosting.

MAKES 8 TO 10 SERVINGS

BERRY ICEBOX CAKE

2 cups strawberries or raspberries

2 tablespoons sugar

1-pound loaf prepared pound cake

½ pint heavy cream

3 large egg yolks

1 cup powdered sugar

½ teaspoon almond extract

In a bowl, sprinkle the berries with the sugar and set aside to draw out some of the juices. Cut the cake lengthwise into ¼-inch slices. Arrange a row of cake slices over the bottom of a 5-by-9-inch loaf pan and cover with the sweetened berries. Add another layer of cake slices and then another of the berries. Add a third layer of cake slices. Beat the cream until thick and stiff. Beat the egg yolks well and gradually add the powdered sugar, beating until thick. Gently stir the egg yolk mixture and almond extract into the beaten cream. Pour over the cake and berries. Chill 3 to 4 hours before serving.

Note: This recipe contains uncooked eggs, which may increase your risk for foodborne illness.

MAKES 8 SERVINGS

BLUEBERRY SUMMER PUDDING

3 cups blueberries

¾ cup brown sugar

½ cup water

Butter, softened

6 slices whole wheat bread

Ground cinnamon

Ground ginger

In a saucepan, mix together the blueberries, sugar, and water and cook for 10 minutes. Lightly butter the bread slices, then lightly sprinkle each with cinnamon and ginger. Beginning with the berries, alternate layers of berries and bread in a loaf pan. The last layer should be berries. Chill in the refrigerator for 4 hours or more.

Unmold and cut into slices to serve.

MAKES 6 SERVINGS

RASPBERRY CAKE

Hannah Weber • Quincy, Washington

Vegetable shortening, for greasing

2 cups all-purpose flour

1½ teaspoons baking powder

½ teaspoon baking soda

¾ cup buttermilk

1 teaspoon vanilla extract

½ cup vegetable shortening

1¼ cups sugar

3 large eggs

2 cups raspberries

½ cup chopped walnuts

Ice cream or whipped cream, for serving

Preheat the oven to 350°F. Grease two 9-inch round cake pans.

Sift together the flour, baking powder, and baking soda. Separately combine the buttermilk and vanilla. In another bowl, cream the shortening and sugar; add the eggs, one at a time, beating after each addition, then beat the batter for 1 minute more. Add the flour mixture, alternating with the buttermilk and vanilla, and beat until mixed. Fold in the raspberries and nuts. Pour the batter into the prepared pans, divining evenly, and bake a toothpick or skewer inserted into the center of the cake comes out clean, 35 to 40 minutes.

The cake may be served warm or cooled, with ice cream or whipped cream. Other wild berries work well in this recipe too.

MAKES 16 SERVINGS

SALMONBERRY CAKE

Nonstick cooking spray,
for greasing

2 cups all-purpose flour

1 teaspoon baking soda

½ teaspoon salt

1 teaspoon ground allspice

1 teaspoon ground cinnamon

1 teaspoon ground nutmeg

¼ cup butter

1 cup sugar

3 large eggs

1 cup salmonberry jam

¾ cup buttermilk

Frosting of your choice
(page 128)

Preheat the oven to 375°F. Grease and flour two 9-inch round cake pans.

Sift together the flour, baking soda, salt, allspice, cinnamon, and nutmeg. In another bowl, cream the butter and sugar together until fluffy. Beat the eggs until light, add them to the sugar mixture, and beat well. Blend the jam and buttermilk together and stir into the egg mixture, alternating with the dry ingredients. Pour the batter into the prepared pans, dividing evenly. Bake until a toothpick or skewer inserted into the center of the cake comes out clean, 20 to 25 minutes. Frost with your favorite frosting.

MAKES 16 SERVINGS

VARIATION: Use raspberry jam in the place of salmonberry jam.

SPICED CRANBERRY CAKE

½ cup vegetable shortening, plus more for greasing

1 cup brown sugar

1 large egg, beaten

1 cup raisins

¾ cup chopped nuts

1¾ cups all-purpose flour

1 teaspoon baking soda

1 teaspoon baking powder

1 teaspoon ground cinnamon

½ teaspoon ground cloves

¼ teaspoon salt

1 cup Whole Berry Cranberry Sauce (page 52)

Cranberry Cheese Frosting (page 128)

Preheat the oven to 350°F. Grease a 10-inch tube pan.

Cream the shortening with the sugar. Add the egg and mix well. Stir in the raisins and nuts. Sift together the flour, baking soda, baking powder, cinnamon, cloves, and salt, add to the shortening mixture, and mix well. Gently stir in the Whole Berry Cranberry Sauce so as not to break the berries. Pour the batter into the prepared tube pan and bake until the top is golden brown and springy to the touch, about 1 hour. Let cool completely on a wire rack.

Frost with the Cranberry Cheese Frosting.

MAKES 8 TO 10 SERVINGS

CRANBERRY-ORANGE UPSIDE-DOWN CAKE

1½ cups lowbush cranberries

2 medium oranges

2 tablespoons butter

1 cup brown sugar

1⅓ cups cake flour

2 teaspoons baking powder

¼ teaspoon salt

¼ cup vegetable shortening

1 to 2 teaspoons finely grated orange zest

¾ cup sugar

1 large egg

¼ cup evaporated milk

¼ cup orange juice

¼ teaspoon ground nutmeg

Preheat the oven to 350°F.

In a bowl, crush the berries. Peel the oranges and divide into sections, removing as much of the membrane as possible. In a saucepan, melt the butter and stir in the brown sugar. Pour the butter mixture into a 9-inch nonstick cake pan. Pour the crushed cranberries into the dish, followed by the orange segments.

Sift together the flour, baking powder, and salt. In another bowl, cream the shortening with the orange zest, gradually add the sugar, and beat until fluffy. Add the egg and beat again. Mix together the milk, orange juice, and nutmeg and add to the shortening mixture, alternating with dry ingredients, a little at a time, beating between additions. Pour the cake batter over the fruit and bake until a toothpick or skewer inserted into the center of the cake comes out clean, 40 to 50 minutes.

Let the cake cool slightly, then carefully invert onto a platter.

MAKES 8 TO 10 SERVINGS

Blueberries and cranberries may be picked and place into large pails, but soft fruits such as raspberries and thimbleberries should be collected in small containers, as they crush easily.

BLUEBERRY CUPCAKES

Hannah Weber • Quincy, Washington

⅓ cup butter

½ cup firmly packed brown sugar

½ cup sugar

1 large egg

1¾ cups all-purpose flour

1 teaspoon baking powder

¼ teaspoon salt

¼ teaspoon ground nutmeg

¼ teaspoon ground cinnamon

½ cup milk

1 cup blueberries (thawed, if frozen)

Sour Cream Frosting (page 128) using dried blueberries

Preheat the oven to 350°F. Line a 12-cup muffin pan with paper liners.

In a bowl, cream together the butter and sugars until light and fluffy. Add the egg and beat well. Sift together the flour, baking powder, salt, nutmeg, and cinnamon. Add this flour mixture to the creamed mixture, alternating with the milk, and mix until blended. Carefully stir in the blueberries, distributing them evenly throughout the batter. Fill the muffin cups half full with the batter. Bake until a toothpick or skewer inserted into the center of the cake comes out clean, 20 to 25 minutes. Let cool completely on a wire rack.

Frost with the frosting and serve.

MAKES 12 CUPCAKES

CURRANT CUPCAKES

¾ cup butter

1¼ cups sugar

4 large eggs

2½ cups all-purpose flour

1 tablespoon baking powder

¼ teaspoon ground nutmeg

⅛ teaspoon salt

¾ cup currants

¾ cup milk

1 teaspoon vanilla extract

Preheat the oven to 350°F. Line a 12-cup muffin pan with paper liners.

In a bowl, cream together the butter and sugar; beat in the eggs one at a time. Sift together the flour, baking powder, nutmeg, and salt; add the currants. Gradually add the dry ingredients and the milk to the creamed mixture. Add the vanilla and mix well.

Fill the muffin cups half full with the batter. Bake until a toothpick or skewer inserted into the center of the cake comes out clean, 20 to 25 minutes. Let cool completely on a wire rack.

MAKES 12 CUPCAKES

ORANGE-CRANBERRY TORTE

Nonstick cooking spray, for greasing

2¼ cups all-purpose flour

1 cup sugar

1 teaspoon baking powder

1 teaspoon baking soda

Pinch of salt

1 cup chopped walnuts

1 cup diced dates

1 cup lowbush cranberries

Finely grated orange zest

2 large eggs, slightly beaten

1 cup buttermilk

⅔ cup vegetable oil

1 cup orange juice

1 cup powdered sugar

Whipped cream, for serving, optional

Preheat the oven to 350°F. Grease and flour a 10-inch tube pan.

Sift together the flour, sugar, baking powder, baking soda, and salt. Stir in the nuts, dates, berries, and orange zest. In a bowl, whisk together the eggs, buttermilk, and oil. Stir the buttermilk mixture into the flour mixture until well blended. Spoon the batter into the prepared pan and bake until the top is golden brown and springy to the touch, about 1 hour. Let cool on a wire rack for 1 hour.

Remove the torte from the pan onto a rack placed over a wide plate. Combine the orange juice and powdered sugar and pour over the torte. Gather the drippings on the plate to pour over the torte again. Set the plate in a dish deeper than the torte, or insert several toothpicks in the top of the torte. Wrap the torte in foil, taking care not to touch the glaze, and refrigerate for 24 hours.

Serve as is or with whipped cream.

MAKES 8 TO 10 SERVINGS

CRAN-APPLE SHORTCAKE

SHORTCAKE

Vegetable shortening,
for greasing

2 cups all-purpose flour

1 tablespoon sugar

4 teaspoons baking powder

½ teaspoon salt

½ cup vegetable shortening

1 large egg, well-beaten

½ cup milk

TOPPING

1 cup finely chopped raw
lowbush cranberries

1 cup peeled and finely
chopped tart apples

¼ cup crushed and drained
pineapple

1 cup sugar

Pinch of salt

Whipped cream, for serving

Preheat the oven to 350°F and grease two 8-inch round cake pans.

Sift the flour, sugar, baking powder, and salt into a bowl. Cut in the shortening until the mixture is crumbly. In another bowl, beat combine the egg and milk, then stir into the flour mixture just enough to moisten well. Turn the mixture onto a lightly floured work surface and lightly bring together with your hands. Divide the dough in half and pat out each half to the diameter of a pan. Place one dough half in each pan. Bake until the shortcakes are golden brown, about 25 minutes. Let cool completely on a wire rack.

For the topping, in a bowl, mix the cranberries, apples, pineapple, sugar, and salt. Let stand for 2 hours.

To serve, spread the fruit generously between and on top of the shortcake rounds, stacking them like a layer cake. Cut the finished cake into wedges and serve with whipped cream.

MAKES 10 TO 12 SERVINGS

VARIATION: Salmonberry Shortcake: For the berry mixture, mix together 3 cups crushed salmonberries, ¾ cup sugar, and 1 tablespoon lemon juice. Let stand for 15 minutes.

STRAWBERRY SHORTCAKE

Virginia Hetland • Olympia, Washington

Nonstick cooking spray, for greasing

3½ cups all-purpose flour

3 tablespoons sugar

3 teaspoons baking powder

½ teaspoon salt

¼ teaspoon ground nutmeg

½ cup vegetable shortening, chilled

1 large egg, well-beaten

¼ cup milk, plus more as needed

Softened butter, for serving

Sweetened strawberries, for serving

Sweetened whipped cream, for serving

Whole strawberries, for garnishing

Preheat the oven to 400°F. Grease 2 baking sheets.

Sift together the flour, sugar, baking powder, salt, and nutmeg. Sift the ingredients again into a bowl. Cut in the shortening until the mixture is crumbly in texture. In a small bowl, combine the egg and milk. Make a well in the flour mixture and add the egg mixture, mixing lightly with a fork to form a soft dough that is a little stiffer than biscuit dough; you may need to mix in a little more milk.

Turn the dough out onto a lightly floured work surface and knead gently for a few seconds. Using a rolling pin, roll out the dough into a ½-inch-thick round. Using a 3-inch round cookie cutter, cut out as many rounds from the dough as possible. Arrange the rounds on the prepared baking sheets, several inches apart, and brush the tops with milk. Bake until well browned, about 15 minutes.

To serve, spread butter over warm rounds and place on serving plates. Pour the strawberries over half the rounds and cover with the remaining rounds and more berries. Top with a spoonful of whipped cream and garnish with a perfect berry or two.

MAKES 12 SERVINGS

CRANBERRY CHEESE FROSTING

1 (3-ounce) package cream cheese, softened

4 tablespoons Lowbush Cranberry Sauce (page 50)

⅛ teaspoon salt

1 pound powdered sugar

In a bowl, mix the cream cheese and with the Lowbush Cranberry Sauce and salt until blended. Gradually stir in powdered sugar until the frosting is creamy in texture. This is not only a good cake icing but also a wonderful after-school treat when spread on graham crackers.

MAKES ABOUT 2 CUPS

SOUR CREAM FROSTING

1 cup sour cream

1 cup sugar

1 cup dried wild berries

Pinch of salt

In the top part of a double boiler, combine the sour cream, sugar, berries, and salt. Place over the bottom part of the double boiler over simmering water and cook, stirring occasionally, until warm and smooth. This is a rich frosting, and you may prefer to use it only as a filling between layers, using another icing to frost your cake.

MAKES ABOUT 2 CUPS

STRAWBERRY CAKE FILLING

⅓ cup powdered sugar

2 cups whipped cream

1 large egg white, stiffly beaten

½ teaspoon vanilla extract

Pinch of salt

½ cup crushed strawberries

In a bowl, gently fold the powdered sugar into whipped cream; fold in the stiffly beaten egg white. Add the vanilla and salt and blend well. Fold in the strawberries and use right away.

Note: This recipe contains uncooked eggs, which may increase your risk for foodborne illness.

MAKES ABOUT 2½ CUPS

VARIATION: You can also try this with wild raspberries or nagoonberries.

COOKIES AND BARS

ALASKA HERMITS

Nonstick cooking spray,
for greasing

½ cup butter, softened

½ cup sugar

½ cup molasses

2 large eggs, well-beaten

½ teaspoon salt

2 cups all-purpose flour

1 teaspoon baking powder

½ teaspoon cream of tartar

1 teaspoon ground cinnamon

½ teaspoon ground cloves

¼ teaspoon ground nutmeg

¼ teaspoon ground mace

¼ cup raisins

¼ cup dried wild currants or
serviceberries

3 tablespoons finely cut
candied orange peel

½ cup nuts (more if desired)

Preheat the oven to 350°F and grease two baking sheets.

In a bowl, cream together the butter and sugar; add the molasses, eggs, and salt and beat well. Sift together 1¾ cups of the flour, the baking powder, cream of tartar, cinnamon, cloves, nutmeg, and mace; add to the butter mixture and mix well. In another bowl, mix together the raisins, berries, orange peel, and nuts; sprinkle with the remaining ¼ cup flour and toss to coat the ingredients. Add the nut mixture to the butter-flour mixture and mix until incorporated.

Drop the batter from a teaspoon onto the prepared baking sheets. The batter should be quite thin, spreading out well on the pans—leave about 2 inches of space between each cookie. Bake until the cookies are firm to the touch, about 15 minutes.

MAKES ABOUT 3 DOZEN

BERRY-OATMEAL COOKIES

Nonstick cooking spray, for greasing

½ cup butter, softened

1½ cups sugar

½ cup molasses

2 large eggs, well-beaten

1¾ cups all-purpose flour

1 teaspoon baking soda

1 teaspoon salt

1 teaspoon ground cinnamon

2 cups rolled oats

1 cup dried watermelon berries

¾ cup coarsely chopped nuts

Preheat the oven to 375°F and grease two baking sheets.

In a bowl, beat together the butter, sugar, molasses, and eggs. In another bowl, combine the flour, baking soda, salt, and cinnamon; sift the mixture twice, then stir it into the butter mixture until blended. Mix in the rolled oats, berries, and nuts. Drop the dough by teaspoonfuls onto the prepared baking sheets. Bake until well browned, 10 to 12 minutes.

MAKES ABOUT 4 DOZEN

VARIATION: If you don't have watermelon berries on hand, use dried salal or serviceberries.

BERRY AND ROSE HIP MACAROONS

Nonstick cooking spray, for greasing

¾ cup dried berries of your choice

¼ cup crushed dried rose hips

7 ounces sweetened condensed milk

2 cups crushed cornflakes

1 cup shredded coconut

½ teaspoon vanilla extract

½ teaspoon dried orange granules

¼ teaspoon salt

Preheat the oven to 300°F. Grease two baking sheets.

In a bowl, mix together the berries, rose hips, condensed milk, cornflakes, coconut, vanilla, orange granules, and salt. Shape the mixture into small, even-size balls with your fingers. Place the dough balls on the prepared baking sheets and bake for 10 minutes. Allow to cool for 2 to 3 minutes before removing from baking sheets.

MAKES ABOUT 2 DOZEN

It only takes a few rose hips to give you all the vitamin C value found in one orange. And the farther north they grow, the more vitamin C the hips have.

CRANBERRY BARS

2½ cups graham cracker crumbs

½ cup butter, melted

1 (3-ounce) package black cherry gelatin

½ cup sugar

1 teaspoon lemon juice

1¼ cups boiling water

2 cups heavy cream

½ to ¾ cup lowbush cranberries

Preheat the oven to 350°F. In a bowl, combine the graham cracker crumbs and butter, blending well. Press the mixture into the bottom of a 9-by-9-inch pan. Bake for 20 minutes, then let cool completely on a wire rack.

In a heatproof bowl, mix the gelatin, sugar, and lemon juice. Add ¼ cup of the boiling water and stir to dissolve the gelatin and sugar. Stir in the remaining 1 cup boiling water. Place in the refrigerator and chill until the gelatin is almost set, but not yet firm, 1 to 2 hours.

In a bowl, whip the cream until soft peaks form and stir in berries; fold into the gelatin. Spread the gelatin-cream mixture on the cooled graham cracker crust. Refrigerate at least 3 hours. Cut into bars or squares for serving.

MAKES 9 TO 12 SERVINGS

FRUIT-NUT COOKIES

Nonstick cooking spray,
for greasing

½ cup butter

1½ cups brown sugar

2 large eggs, slightly beaten

2 tablespoons buttermilk

½ cup chopped walnuts

1 cup finely chopped
dried wild currants

½ cup dried berries of
your choice, chopped

½ teaspoon ground nutmeg

½ teaspoon ground
cinnamon

3 cups all-purpose flour

1 teaspoon baking soda

Preheat the oven to 350°F and grease two baking sheets.

In a bowl, mix together the butter and ¼ cup of the brown sugar. Slowly blend in the eggs and buttermilk. Gradually add the remaining 1¼ cups sugar, then the walnuts, currants, berries, nutmeg, and cinnamon. In another bowl, mix together the flour and baking soda and gradually add it to the berry mixture, beating after each addition. Drop the dough from a teaspoon onto the prepared baking sheets. Bake until the cookie edges are brown, about 15 minutes. Remove from the oven and allow to cool a little, then transfer to wire racks to cool completely.

MAKES 3 TO 4 DOZEN

GLAZED COOKIE BARS

1 (17-ounce) package
purchased cookie dough,
well chilled

1 (8-ounce) package
whipped cream cheese

Assorted wild berries,
as needed (blueberries and
salmonberries make
a nice combination)

½ cup orange marmalade

2 tablespoons water

Preheat the oven to 375°F. Line a baking sheet with foil.

Cut the cookie dough into ⅛-inch-thick slices. Arrange the dough slices on the foil so they overlap slightly, making a rectangle approximately 14 by 10 inches. Press the overlapping portions slightly to seal. Bake until browned, 10 to 12 minutes.

Let cool completely, then remove the foil. Spread the cream cheese over the rectangle and sprinkle generously with wild berries.

In a saucepan, mix together the marmalade and water and warm over low heat until smooth. Glaze the top of the cookie rectangle with this mixture and chill for several hours. Cut into squares or bars.

MAKES 24 BARS

LINZER SLICES

Nonstick cooking spray, for greasing

3 large eggs

2¼ cups sugar

¾ cup butter, melted

3½ cups all-purpose flour

1 teaspoon baking powder

¼ teaspoon salt

2 teaspoons ground cinnamon

1 teaspoon ground cloves

Finely grated zest and juice of 1 lemon

Strawberry preserves

Preheat the oven to 375°F and grease a baking sheet.

In a bowl, beat 2 of the eggs until light in color. Gradually beat in 1½ cups of the sugar. Mix in the melted butter. In another bowl, sift together the flour, baking powder, salt, cinnamon, and cloves and mix into the egg-butter mixture. Mix in the lemon zest and juice. Turn the dough out onto a floured work surface and knead until smooth. Cover the dough with plastic wrap and let stand for 2 or more hours.

Using a rolling pin, roll out the dough to a ½-inch-thick rectangle. Using a large knife, cut the dough into 1½-by-10-inch strips. With the handle of a wooden spoon, make a groove down the middle of each strip. Fill the groove with strawberry preserves, and place the filled strips on the prepared baking sheet. Bake until brown, about 15 minutes.

In a bowl, beat together the remaining egg and remaining ¾ cup of sugar to make a glaze. Brush the glaze over the baked strips while they're still hot. Cut at once into diagonal pieces or squares. Linzer Slices is a super holiday confection!

MAKES ABOUT 24 BARS

STRAWBERRY BARS

2 cups all-purpose flour

½ teaspoon ground ginger

¼ teaspoon salt

¾ cup cold butter,
cut into pieces

8 ounces cold cream cheese,
cut into pieces

1 large egg yolk,
beaten

Nonstick cooking spray,
for greasing

¼ cup strawberry preserves

1 large egg white,
lightly beaten

Sugar

In a bowl, mix together the flour, ginger, and salt. Using a pastry blender, two forks, or your fingertips, blend in the butter and cream cheese until the mixture is even and crumbly. Stir in the egg yolk and then gently knead the dough until smooth. Divide the dough into thirds. Form each third into a rectangle, wrap in plastic wrap, and chill until firm, at least 2 hours.

Preheat the oven to 375°F and grease a baking sheet. On a lightly floured work surface, roll out the chilled rectangle ¼ inch thick, then transfer to the prepared baking sheet.

Spoon a strip of berry preserves down one side of the rectangle. Brush the egg white along the edges of the dough, then fold the dough over to form a long, enclosed bar. Cut slits in the top and crimp the edges by pressing with a floured fork.

Repeat to roll out, fill, and seal the remaining dough rectangles. Brush the tops of the dough with egg white and sprinkle lightly with sugar. Bake until golden brown about 20 minutes. Let stand to cool, then cut into 1½-inch bars.

MAKES ABOUT 2 DOZEN

FROZEN AND CHILLED DESSERTS

FROZEN CRANBERRY TORTE

2 cups Lowbush Cranberry Sauce (page 50)

2 tablespoons lemon juice

½ pint heavy cream

¼ cup powdered sugar

1 teaspoon vanilla extract

⅔ cup chopped pecans or walnuts

In a bowl, mix together the Lowbush Cranberry Sauce and lemon juice and pour into a 6-by-9-inch loaf pan. Do not fill the pan more than halfway. Whip the cream until soft peaks form, then fold in the sugar, vanilla, and nuts. Spread this mixture over the cranberry layer and freeze until firm. This may be prepared for a party several days ahead and kept frozen. Cut into slices to serve.

MAKES 8 TO 10 SERVINGS

FROZEN BERRY FLUFF

Mrs. Westcott Gaines • North Little Rock, Arkansas

1 cup heavy cream

3 ounces purchased marshmallow fluff

¾ cup your choice of crushed berries

¼ cup chopped nuts

In a bowl, whip the cream until stiff peaks form and gently but thoroughly fold in the marshmallow fluff. Fold in the crushed berries and nuts. Pour the mixture into a shallow casserole dish and freeze until semifirm. This easy treat has a velvety texture and is especially good served between waffles with fruit syrup on top.

MAKES 4 TO 6 SERVINGS

FRESH BERRY ICE CREAM

4 cups half-and-half, well chilled

2 cups cold water

2 (14-ounce) cans sweetened condensed milk, well chilled

2 tablespoons vanilla extract

3 cups your choice of crushed berries, well chilled

If necessary, pre-chill your ice cream maker according to the manufacturer's instructions.

In a large bowl with a spout, mix together the half-and-half, water, sweetened condensed milk, vanilla, and berries. Pour the mixture into the ice cream maker and churn according to the manufacturer's instructions (you may need to do this in batches; refrigerate any milk mixture until needed). Transfer the ice cream to freezer containers and freeze until firm.

MAKES ABOUT 2 QUARTS

FROZEN STRAWBERRY CUSTARD

2 large egg yolks, beaten

1¼ cups powdered sugar

1 tablespoon lemon juice

2 cups fresh strawberries

2 large egg whites

½ cup whipped cream

In a bowl, whisk together the egg yolks and ¾ cup of the powdered sugar until thick and creamy. In another bowl, mix together the lemon juice and berries, and then stir into the egg yolk mixture. In a clean bowl, whisk the egg whites with the remaining ½ cup powdered sugar, beating vigorously until stiff peaks form. Fold the egg whites and whipped cream into the fruit mixture. Place in a freezer until firm. Allow to stand at room temperature for 5 to 10 minutes before serving.

Note: This recipe contains uncooked eggs, which may increase your risk for foodborne illness.

MAKES ABOUT 1 QUART

LOWBUSH CRANBERRY PARFAIT

1 envelope unflavored
gelatin

6 tablespoons sugar, plus
more to taste if desired

2 large egg yolks

1½ cups milk

1 teaspoon vanilla extract

2 (8-ounce) packages cream
cheese, softened

2 large egg whites

2 cups canned lowbush
cranberries, chilled

In a saucepan, combine the gelatin and 2 tablespoons of the sugar. In a bowl, beat the egg yolks with the milk, then add to the gelatin mixture. Stir the mixture over low heat until the gelatin dissolves, about 5 minutes. Remove from the heat and stir in the vanilla. In another bowl, beat the cream cheese until smooth, then gradually beat in the gelatin mixture. Chill, stirring occasionally, until the mixture forms a mound when dropped from a spoon.

In a clean bowl, beat the egg whites until soft peaks form, then beat in the remaining 4 tablespoons sugar until stiff. (Add extra sugar to taste at this stage if your berries are particularly tart.) Fold this into the cream cheese mixture. Alternate layers of the cream cheese mixture and berries in parfait or other dessert dishes. Chill until set.

Note: This recipe contains uncooked eggs, which may increase your risk for foodborne illness.

MAKES 6 SERVINGS

LOWBUSH CRANBERRY SHERBET

2 cups lowbush cranberries

1½ cups cold water

1 cup sugar

1 teaspoon unflavored gelatin

Juice of 1 lemon

Simmer the cranberries in 1¼ cups of the cold water, stirring frequently, for 5 minutes. Force the berries through a fine sieve to make a puree. Return the puree to the saucepan and add the sugar. Stir over medium heat until all the sugar is dissolved, then simmer gently for 5 minutes more.

Soak the gelatin in the remaining ¼ cup cold water until the gelatin dissolves, about 1 minute. Stir in the lemon juice. Stir the gelatin mixture into the berry puree and allow to cool. Freeze in ice-cube trays until firm. Remove from refrigerator and break into small chunks in the bowl of an electric mixer. Beat until the mixture is mushy, allowing plenty of air to build up in the sherbet to make a light texture. Put the mixture back into ice-cube trays again and freeze until firm.

To serve, quickly break up the ice cubes in a blender or food processor and spoon into bowls. This is excellent with fruit salad on a hot day.

MAKES ABOUT 1 QUART

RASPBERRY ICE

Lois Smith • Olympia, Washington

2 quarts wild raspberries
2 cups sugar
2 cups water
1 tablespoon lemon juice
Pinch of salt

Put the berries in a bowl and sprinkle with the sugar. Cover and allow to stand for about 2 hours. Using a wooden spoon, crush the berries thoroughly and then force them through a fine sieve to make a puree. Stir in the water, lemon juice, and salt, and pour into ice-cube trays to freeze.

To serve, quickly break up the ice cubes in a blender or food processor and spoon into bowls.

MAKES ABOUT 1 QUART

VARIATION: Substitute strawberries for the raspberries.

A few fresh, unsweetened blueberries or raspberries added to ice cream just before serving make an especially appealing dessert in warm weather. Sweeten them a bit if you must, but they are most refreshing if unsweetened.

FROZEN RASPBERRY-MARSHMALLOW BARS

Hannah Weber • Quincy, Washington

2 cups miniature
marshmallows

1 cup milk

1 pint heavy cream

2 cups raspberries

25 graham cracker squares

Put the marshmallows and milk in the top part of a double boiler. Place over the bottom part of the double boiler filled with simmering water and heat, stirring occasionally, until melted. Set aside to cool.

In a bowl, whip the cream until stiff peaks form and then fold in the berries. Add the cooled marshmallow mixture and fold gently but thoroughly. In another bowl, crumble the graham crackers into crumbs.

Line a 9-by-13-inch pan with three-quarters of the crumbs. Pour the marshmallow-berries mixture over the top. Sprinkle the remaining crumbs evenly over the top. Chill until serving time. This may also be prepared ahead of time and kept frozen. Remove from the freezer an hour before serving. Cut into rectangles to serve.

MAKES 10 TO 12 SERVINGS

FROZEN STRAWBERRY MOUSSE

Betty Ryan • Seattle, Washington

2 cups strawberries

¾ cup sugar

1 tablespoon lemon juice

Pinch of salt

1 cup heavy cream

In a bowl, combine the berries and sugar. Use a wooden spoon to crush the berries well. Stir in the lemon juice and salt. In another bowl, whip the cream until stiff peaks form. Fold the berries into the whipped cream. Transfer the mixture to a shallow casserole dish and freeze for about 2 hours, stirring once during that time. Spoon into bowls to serve.

MAKES 6 TO 8 SERVINGS

STRAWBERRY SWIRL

1 cup graham cracker
crumbs

3 tablespoons sugar

¼ cup melted butter

2 cups crushed strawberries

1 (3-ounce) package
strawberry gelatin

1 cup boiling water

Water

½ pound marshmallows

½ cup milk

1 cup whipped cream

In a bowl, mix together the graham cracker crumbs, 1 tablespoon of the sugar, and the butter and press into a 9-by-9-inch pan. Place in the refrigerator.

In another bowl, sprinkle the remaining 2 tablespoons sugar over the berries and let stand for 30 minutes.

In a medium bowl, dissolve the gelatin in the boiling water. Drain the strawberries, reserving the juice. Add enough water to the juice to make 1 cup of liquid, then stir into the gelatin mixture and chill until partially set. Meanwhile, in a saucepan, combine the marshmallows and milk and warm over low heat until the marshmallows melt, stirring to prevent scorching. Cool thoroughly, then fold in the whipped cream. Add the berries to the cooled gelatin mixture, then swirl in the marshmallow-whipped cream mixture to create a marbled effect. Pour into the crust and chill until set, 3 to 4 hours minutes. Cut into squares for serving.

MAKES 8 TO 10 SERVINGS

THIMBLEBERRY WHIP

Approximately 1 quart
thimbleberries, plus more for
layering if desired

½ cup sugar

Pinch of salt

2 large egg whites

1 tablespoon lemon juice

Force the thimbleberries through a fine sieve until you have 1 cup of puree. Pour the puree into a saucepan, add the sugar and salt, and warm over medium-low heat, stirring, until the sugar is dissolved. Let cool.

In a clean bowl, beat the egg whites until stiff peaks form. Gradually pour the cooled berry mixture over the stiffly beaten egg whites, beating constantly. Mix in the lemon juice. Spoon the mixture into parfait glasses, layering it with fresh whole berries, if you like. Chill before serving.

Note: This recipe contains uncooked eggs, which may increase your risk for foodborne illness.

MAKES 4 SERVINGS

WILD BERRY ICE

2 cups hot water

2 cups sugar

2 cups wild berries

¾ cup berry juice

In a saucepan, combine the hot water and sugar; stir over medium-high heat until the sugar is dissolved. Boil for 5 minutes without stirring, then allow to cool. Crush the berries and drain and reserve the juice. Add the crushed berries and ¾ cup juice to the sugar syrup. Pour into ice-cube trays and freeze until firm.

To serve, quickly break up the ice cubes in a blender or food processor and spoon into bowls.

MAKES ABOUT 1 QUART

VARIATION: Wild raspberries or black raspberries, lowbush cranberries, or blueberries may be used in this recipe. If you try cranberries, use more sugar.

WILD BERRY PARFAIT

Wild strawberries or raspberries

Sugar to taste

Finely grated zest of 1 orange

Vanilla ice cream

Whipped cream, for serving

Crush the berries slightly. Add the sugar and orange zest and stir to mingle the flavors. Place a layer of ice cream in the bottom of a parfait glass, then a layer of the prepared berries. Alternate layers of ice cream and fruit until glass is full. Freeze. When it is time to serve, drop a dollop of whipped cream on top. Other berries are excellent prepared in this fashion—try a combination of your favorites.

SERVINGS VARY

CANDIES

BLUEBERRY COCONUT CLUSTERS

1 cup shredded coconut

2 tablespoons butter, softened

1 small egg

1 teaspoon vanilla extract

½ teaspoon ground nutmeg

Pinch of salt

1 cup powdered sugar, plus more as needed

½ cup blueberry puree

Preheat the oven to 325°F. Spread the coconut on a rimmed baking sheet and toast in the oven until light brown, 5 to 10 minutes.

Put the butter in a bowl and stir in the unbeaten egg, vanilla, nutmeg, and salt until blended. Gradually stir in ½ cup of the powdered sugar. Add the blueberry puree and the remaining ½ cup of powdered sugar and beat thoroughly. Set aside about ¼ cup of the toasted coconut and add the remaining ¾ cup coconut to the bowl. Stir well, adding enough additional powdered sugar to make a very stiff mixture.

Transfer the mass to a large sheet of waxed paper sprinkled liberally with powdered sugar. Knead the candy as you would bread dough, adding more sugar if necessary to keep it from sticking. Pinch off small bits of the candy and roll between your palms to form balls the size of large marbles. Place the balls on a clean sheet of waxed paper and sprinkle the ¼ cup coconut set aside earlier on top of each ball. Press down the center of each candy with your thumb to make an indentation. Let stand until the top is dry, then turn the balls over to dry the other side. Store in an airtight container with waxed paper between the layers.

MAKES 24 TO 36 CLUSTERS

CANDIED ROSE HIPS

½ cup sugar, plus more
for finishing

¼ cup water

1½ cups ripe rose hips,
cleaned

In a saucepan, mix the ½ cup sugar with the water and boil briefly to make a syrup. Add the rose hips and boil gently until the fruit is soft, 10 to 12 minutes. Using a slotted skimmer, lift the rose hips from the syrup and set aside on waxed paper to drain. While the rose hips are still moist, dust them with sugar. If possible, dry the rose hips slowly in the sun; if not possible, dry them in an oven set at its lowest temperature, being sure to leave the oven door ajar so moisture can escape. Add more sugar if the candy is sticky.

Store the candied rose hips in an airtight metal container with waxed paper between the layers. Candied Rose Hips can be used with, or in place of, nuts and raisins in cookies, in puddings with grated lemon zest, in upside-down cakes, or as snacks.

MAKES ABOUT 1½ CUPS

FRUIT SQUARES

1 cup sugar

2 large eggs, beaten

¼ teaspoon salt

1 cup chopped dried berries

2 cups finely chopped shredded coconut

2½ cups puffed rice cereal

¾ cup chopped almonds

1 teaspoon vanilla extract

Toasted coconut

In a bowl, mix together the sugar, eggs, and salt; blend in the dried berries and shredded coconut. Pour the mixture into a skillet and cook slowly for 10 to 15 minutes, stirring constantly. Remove from heat and add the cereal, almonds, and vanilla, mixing well. Let stand for 15 minutes. Spread the cooled mixture in an 8-by-8-inch pan. Using a very sharp knife, cut the candy into 1-inch squares and dredge each square in toasted coconut.

MAKES ABOUT 64 SQUARES

Be sure you know your berry identification. Baneberries are definitely poisonous and must be avoided—both the white and the red forms.

WILD BERRY PATTIES

1 large egg yolk

2 tablespoons butter

Finely grated orange zest or dried orange peel granules to taste

¼ cup Lowbush Cranberry Juice (page 160)

Powdered sugar, as needed

In a bowl, mix together the egg yolk, butter, and orange zest. Stir in the cranberry juice. Gradually stir in powdered sugar until the mixture becomes too stiff to stir anymore. Transfer the mixture to a surface liberally dusted with powdered sugar. Knead the candy as you would dough, working in as much of the powdered sugar as it will take. Pinch off small bits of the candy, roll them into even balls, and space them 1 inch apart on waxed paper. Press your thumb into the center of each ball to make a hollow indentation. Let the patties stand overnight to dry; turn the patties over to dry the other side.

Note: This recipe contains uncooked eggs, which may increase your risk for foodborne illness.

SERVINGS VARY

JUICES AND BEVERAGES

LOWBUSH CRANBERRY JUICE

Lowbush cranberries
Water

In a saucepan, mix 2 parts cranberries with 1 part water and boil gently until the berries soften, about 5 minutes. Crush and strain the mixture through a wet jelly bag to obtain a clear juice. Reserve the pulp for use in jams or desserts. Seal the juice in sterilized bottles or canning jars for later use in beverages, jellies, and sauces.

SERVINGS VARY

ROSE HIP JUICE

Rose hips
Water

If possible, gather your rose hips before the first frost. Clean them well and remove the tails. Place the rose hips in a kettle with enough water to completely cover the fruit. Bring to a boil slowly, reduce the heat, and simmer until the fruit is soft, about 15 minutes. Strain the rose hips through a wet jelly bag overnight. Pour the extracted juice into a container you can cover, then store it in the refrigerator, where it will keep for several weeks. Rose hip juice is ideal to have on hand throughout the preserving season.

SERVINGS VARY

FINLAND-STYLE BERRY SHAKE

2 cups crushed strawberries

2 cups cold milk

1½ tablespoons sugar or honey

If you're using frozen berries, drain off the syrup and reserve it for another use. Pour the strawberries, milk, and sugar or honey into a mixing bowl. Beat for a minute or two with a whisk or hand mixer. Pour into tall drinking glasses and serve. Other wild berries may be used this way, too, but you may need to add more sugar for tarter berries.

MAKES 2 TO 4 SHAKES

RASPBERRY MILKSHAKE

1 cup raspberries

4½ cups cold milk

1 cup instant nonfat milk powder

1 quart vanilla ice cream

Mint leaves

Crush the raspberries. In a large bottle, combine the raspberries, milk, and milk powder. Shake vigorously to blend well. Add the ice cream and shake some more until the ingredients are thoroughly blended. Pour into tall, frosted glasses and garnish with mint leaves.

MAKES 6 TO 8 SERVINGS

VARIATION: Try this basic milkshake recipe with nagoonberries, strawberries, or salmonberries.

ALASKA CRANBERRY TEA

Rachel Adkins • North Pole, Alaska

1 quart lowbush cranberries
2 cinnamon sticks
3 quarts water
2 cups sugar
2 cups orange juice
6 tablespoons lemon juice

In a saucepan, combine the cranberries, cinnamon sticks, and water and simmer until the berries are tender, about 5 minutes. Strain. Add the sugar, orange juice, and lemon juice and simmer until the sugar is dissolved. Serve hot.

MAKES 6 TO 8 SERVINGS

A bit of lemon juice or zest adds depth to blueberry dishes. Orange juice or zest are natural complements in any cranberry recipe.

OLD-FASHIONED ALASKA PUNCH

1 cup lowbush cranberries

1 cup ripe rose hips, cleaned

½ cup water

1 cup raspberries

1 cup sugar

Pinch of salt

Orange slices

In a saucepan, combine the cranberries, rose hips, and water and simmer until the fruit is soft, about 10 minutes. Add the raspberries and simmer until soft, about 5 minutes. Drain through a wet jelly bag, squeezing it to remove all of the juice. Pour the juice through the jelly bag one more time, but do not squeeze the bag the second time, and just let it drain. Add the sugar and salt and swirl briefly until all the sugar is dissolved. Pour the juice over cracked ice in tall glasses. Float a thin slice of orange on top of each glass.

MAKES 4 TO 6 SERVINGS

CRANBERRY PUNCH

½ cup sugar

2½ cups water

1 quart Lowbush Cranberry Juice (page 160)

1 cup orange juice

Juice of ½ lemon

1 quart ginger ale or soda water

In a saucepan, combine the sugar and ½ cup of the water and boil for 5 minutes. Remove from the heat and set aside to cool. In a pitcher, mix together the syrup, the cranberry, orange, and lemon juice, and the remaining 2 cups water and chill thoroughly. Just before serving, add ginger ale or soda water.

MAKES 8 TO 10 SERVINGS

HUCKLEBERRY NECTAR

1 quart huckleberries
1 quart water
1 cup sugar
Juice of 2 lemons
1 quart soda water

In a saucepan, combine the huckleberries and water and simmer until soft, about 10 minutes. Force the berries through a sieve into the saucepan and stir in the sugar. Simmer for 5 minutes more. Strain the pulp through a jelly bag. Chill thoroughly. To serve, pour the lemon juice over ice cubes in a punch bowl and add the huckleberry juice. Pour in the soda water.

MAKES 10 TO 12 SERVINGS

VARIATIONS:

- Add a little Lowbush Cranberry Juice (page 160) or orange and pineapple juice.
- Use blueberries instead of huckleberries.

BERRY SHRUB

2 quarts cider vinegar

4 quarts raspberries or strawberries, cleaned but not washed

Sugar, as needed

Mint sprigs

In a large stainless steel saucepan, combine the vinegar and berries and let stand for 24 hours. Strain and measure the resulting liquid. Add 1½ pounds sugar for each quart of liquid and boil gently for 30 minutes. Skim any impurities from the top of the liquid and allow to cool in the pan. When cool, pour into sterilized bottles and cap for future use.

When you're ready to serve, pour 3 tablespoons of the berry-vinegar mixture into tea tall glass and fill with ice and water or club soda. Garnish with a sprig of mint and serve with a straw.

MAKES 10 TO 12 SERVINGS

BON VOYAGE PUNCH

2 quarts strawberries

Juice of 1 lemon

2 (750 ml) bottles dry white wine

2 (750 ml) bottles sparkling white wine

Large block of ice

Mint sprigs

In a bowl, combine the berries, lemon juice, and 1 bottle of dry white wine. Chill for several hours. Chill the second bottle of wine and the sparkling wine at the same time. When it's nearly time to serve, place the ice in a large punch bowl. Combine all the liquids in the punch bowl and add a few sprigs of mint. Ladle out the punch with a strawberry in each serving.

MAKES 12 TO 16 SERVINGS

STRAWBERRY-WINE PUNCH

Hannah Weber • Quincy, Washington

½ cup water

1 cup sugar

2 cups strained orange juice

½ cup lemon juice

2 cups fresh whole strawberries

2 cups Rosé wine

1 quart sparkling water

In a saucepan, combine the water and sugar and boil until syrupy, about 5 minutes. Let cool slightly, then stir together with the orange juice, lemon juice, and berries. Pour the mixture over ice in a punch bowl. Add the wine and stir in the sparkling water. Ladle into cups to serve.

MAKES 10 TO 12 SERVINGS

Many people go for drives in the summertime and the drive could well end at a good berry patch. Make it a point always to carry a pail or two and a few strong plastic bags in your car so that when you do happen onto a good patch you will have something to use for picking the berries.
—Alaska Wild Berry Trails

CHRISTMAS CORDIAL

6 cups Lowbush Cranberry
Juice (page 160)

6 cups sugar

4 cups lemon-lime soda

3 cups vodka

In a saucepan, combine the juice and sugar. Bring quickly to a boil and boil until syrupy, 5 to 6 minutes. Let cool until lukewarm. Stir in the soda and vodka and chill in the refrigerator for a few hours before serving.

MAKES 16 TO 20 SERVINGS

TRAIL FOODS AND PRESERVES

BERRY LEATHER

Nonstick cooking spray, for greasing

2 cups your choice of crushed berries

3 tablespoons sugar

Preheat the oven to 140°F to 150°F. Lightly grease a baking sheet.

In a saucepan, mix together the berries and sugar. Bring to a rolling boil over high heat. Reduce the heat to medium and cook, stirring constantly, until syrupy, about 45 minutes. Force the berry mixture through a sieve to remove the seeds; allow to cool slightly. Pour or ladle the berry mixture into 6-inch-wide strips down the length of the prepared baking sheet. Place in the oven, leaving the oven door ajar to allow moisture to escape, until the puree is firm to the touch, 5 to 6 hours.

Peel the berry leather off the pan. If it adheres to the baking sheet, it's not ready to be removed! Roll up the strips in plastic wrap for storage. It keeps about month at room temperature and longer in the freezer.

SERVINGS VARY

Our kids need something besides, or in place of, candy bars and potato chips. Be a wise parent and make your family some Berry Leather as a treat. Berry Leather is not as tough to make as it sounds. It is a slightly tart, nutritious snack made from fresh or dried fruits.
—Mary Alice Griffis • The Nome Nugget

NAGOONBERRY HARDTACK

Nonstick cooking spray, for greasing

4 cups nagoonberries

1 cup shredded coconut

1 cup rolled oats

¼ cup sugar

2 cups all-purpose flour

Preheat the oven to 250°F. Grease a large baking sheet.

In a bowl, mash the berries thoroughly. Mix in the coconut and rolled oats, then the sugar. Stir in the flour until the dough is firm. Drop by spoonfuls onto the prepared baking sheet. Flatten each mound with the bottom of a glass. Bake until firm, about 20 minutes. The end product is a hard, semisweet cookie that's perfect for packing on the trail or for camping.

MAKES 24 TO 36 SERVINGS

VARIATIONS:
- Substitute an equal amount of honey for sugar.
- Substitute an equal amount of cornmeal for flour.

APPLE-MOUNTAIN ASH JELLY

4 pounds mountain ash
berries

4 pounds tart apples,
quartered and cored

Water, as needed

Sugar, as needed

Mint sprigs, if desired

Put the berries and apples in separate saucepans with just enough water to cover them and bring to a boil. Allow them to simmer until soft, about 10 minutes for berries and 15 minutes for apples. Strain them separately through damp jelly bags. Measure equal parts of each juice into a large saucepan. Add 1 cup of sugar for each cup of the mixture; add a sprig of mint, too, if available. Boil the juice to the jelly stage (see page 192), which should take about 10 minutes. Pour the jelly into hot sterilized jelly glasses and seal with lids. Process for 15 minutes in a boiling water bath.

MAKES ABOUT 5 QUARTS

HIGHBUSH CRANBERRY JELLY

University of Alaska Cooperative Extension Service

4 cups highbush cranberries

3 cups water

Sugar

In a saucepan, combine the berries and water and bring to a simmer for a few seconds. Increase the heat so that the mixture boils rapidly for 5 minutes. Strain through a damp jelly bag or several layers of cheesecloth. Measure the juice into the saucepan and add ⅔ cup sugar for each cup of juice. Bring to a boil and stir until the jelly stage is reached (see page 192). Pour into hot, sterilized jelly glasses and seal with lids. Process for 15 minutes in a boiling water bath.

MAKES ABOUT 1 QUART

Highbush cranberries are best when picked slightly underripe, as they become bitter as they ripen.

LOWBUSH CRANBERRY JELLY

2 quarts lowbush cranberries

4 cups water

5 cups sugar

In a saucepan, boil the cranberries in the water for 5 minutes. Strain the berries through a moist jelly bag, squeezing from time to time to extract as much juice as possible. Allow the juice to settle for an hour or so and again strain through the jelly bag, without squeezing this time, to ensure a clear jelly. Return to the saucepan, add the sugar, and bring to a boil. As soon as the mixture comes to a boil, remove it from the heat ladle into hot, sterilized jelly glasses, and seal with lids. Process for 15 minutes in a boiling water bath.

MAKES ABOUT 2 QUARTS

VARIATION: Spiced Cranberry Jelly: Add a 2-inch cinnamon stick, 24 whole cloves, and 6 whole allspice berries during the initial berry cooking.

QUICK LOWBUSH CRANBERRY JELLY

University of Alaska Cooperative Extension Service

1 quart lowbush cranberries

2½ cups water

3 cups sugar

3 ounces liquid pectin

In a saucepan, boil the cranberries in the water for 5 minutes. Strain the mixture through a jelly bag, squeezing hard. Let settle and strain again (without squeezing this time) to ensure a clear jelly. You should have about 3 cups of juice. Add the sugar and pectin, following the directions on the package. Pour into hot, sterilized jelly glasses and seal with lids. Process for 15 minutes in a boiling water bath. Store in a cool place.

MAKES ABOUT 1 QUART

CRANBUTTER

Maureen Wright • May Creek, Alaska

6 cups highbush cranberry puree

4 cups sugar

1 tablespoon ground cinnamon

1½ teaspoons ground allspice

½ teaspoon ground nutmeg

Put the cranberry puree in a large saucepan and add the sugar, cinnamon, allspice, and nutmeg. Cook over medium heat, stirring frequently, for 30 minutes. Pour into sterilized jars and seal immediately. This cranbutter can be made with the fruit puree left over from preparing Highbush Cranberry Jelly (page 173).

MAKES ABOUT 1½ QUARTS

LOWBUSH CRANBERRY MARMALADE

2 oranges

1 lemon

1¾ cups water

⅛ teaspoon baking soda

4 cups lowbush cranberries

6½ cups sugar

3 ounces liquid pectin

Quarter the oranges and lemon, remove the seeds, and cut the fruits into large pieces; do not remove the peels. Chop the fruit finely in a food processor. In a saucepan, combine the chopped citrus, water, and baking soda. Simmer, covered, for 20 minutes, stirring occasionally. Add the berries and continue simmering, covered, for another 10 minutes. Measure exactly 5 cups of the prepared fruit into a large saucepan and add the sugar. Bring to a full, rolling boil for 1 minute. Remove from heat and stir in the pectin all at once. Skim and stir for about 5 minutes, allowing the marmalade to cool slightly. Ladle into hot, sterilized, canning jars and seal with lids. Process for 15 minutes in a boiling water bath.

MAKES ABOUT 1¼ QUARTS

ROSE HIP JELLY

2 cups rose hips, cleaned

2 cups water

4 tablespoons lemon juice

Sugar, as needed

In a saucepan, combine the rose hips and water. Bring to a boil and cook until they are soft, about 10 minutes. Force the rose hips through a coarse sieve and drain through a jelly bag. Measure the juice into a saucepan and add the lemon juice. Add ¾ as much sugar as you have juice. Boil rapidly for 10 minutes and test for the jelly stage (see page 192). If the test is negative, continue cooking the juice until it jells. Pour into hot, sterilized jelly glasses and seal at once with lids. Process for 15 minutes in a boiling water bath.

MAKES 1 TO 2 PINTS

The University of Alaska Cooperative Extension Service recommends freezing wild berries before extracting the juice for jelly making. Freezing prior to extracting yields more juice.

RASPBERRY-CURRANT PRESERVES

Hannah Weber • Quincy, Washington

2 pounds red currants

Water

4 pounds raspberries

Sugar

Wash the currants and simmer for 15 minutes in enough water to prevent the berries from scorching. Drain through a damp jelly bag. Wash the raspberries, but only if really necessary, and place them in a large saucepan. Pour the currant juice over the raspberries and gently heat for 5 minutes. Measure the fruit mixture and add 1 cup sugar for each 2 cups. Simmer the mixture until it jells (see page 192), about 10 minutes. Stir as carefully as possible so the berries will not be crushed. Pour into hot, sterilized canning jars and seal with lids. Process in a boiling water bath for 15 minutes.

MAKES ABOUT 1½ QUARTS

SALMONBERRY PRESERVES

University of Alaska Cooperative Extension Service

Salmonberries

Sugar

In a saucepan, combine equal amounts of salmonberries and sugar and cook the mixture slowly for 15 minutes. Remove from the heat. Using a slotted spoon, transfer the berries to a dish. Boil the remaining juice hard for 15 minutes, then remove from heat. Stir the berries back into the hot juice. Spoon the preserves into hot, sterilized, canning jars and seal with lids. Process for 15 minutes in a boiling water bath.

SERVINGS VARY

SPICED CURRANTS

1½ pounds currants

1 pound brown sugar

1 cup mild cider vinegar

1 teaspoon ground cinnamon

1 teaspoon ground cloves

1 teaspoon ground allspice, optional

Wash the currants, removing the stems. Place in a saucepan, add the brown sugar, vinegar, cinnamon, cloves, and allspice, if using, and heat to the boiling point. Reduce the heat to low and simmer slowly for 1 hour, stirring to prevent sticking. Pour into hot, sterilized canning jars and seal with lids. Process for 15 minutes in a boiling water bath.

MAKES ABOUT 1½ CUPS

WILD CURRANT PRESERVES

3 pounds wild currants

3 pounds sugar

Clean and sort currants, then put them in a saucepan. Cook the fruit slowly over low heat until the juice flows freely. Stir in the sugar and then boil the mixture rapidly for 20 minutes. Pour into hot, sterilized, canning jars and seal with lids. Process for 15 minutes in a boiling water bath.

MAKES ABOUT 1½ QUARTS

Overripe berries should never be used when preserving whole fruits. Use them instead in jams or fruit butters.

ESKIMO AND NATIVE AMERICAN DISHES

AKUTAQ

1 cup vegetable shortening or lard

½ cup seal oil (if seal oil is not available, use vegetable oil)

¼ to ½ cup sugar depending on taste

2½ to 3 cups boned fish, boiled and squeezed dry

4 cups wild berries

Put shortening into large bowl. Squeeze and flatten with the hands until smooth and soft; then add oil to make it even smoother. Mix and blend with hands until soft enough. Add sugar and mix well. Then add the fish, little by little, crumbling and scattering it as you add it until all the fish is in the mixture. At this point the akutaq should be fluffy, like whipped cream. Add the berries as you did the fish. After all is done, freeze until firm. More sugar may be added when served. Most Eskimos have the ingredients for akutaq readily available.

SERVINGS VARY

NATIVE AMERICAN ICE CREAM

Karen Clark • Cassiar, British Columbia

Soopolallie berries

Sugar

Water

In a bowl, mix the berries with sugar to taste and a small amount of water. Use your hands to mix vigorously until the mixture resembles whipped cream, adding more water as needed. This dish is from the Natives of British Columbia, the Yukon, and Alaska. The raw berry, also known as a soapberry, is very bitter due to the presence of saponin.

SERVINGS VARY

OUR FAVORITE ESKIMO ICE CREAM

Audrey Rearden • Homer, Alaska

½ to ¾ cup vegetable shortening

Sugar

1 to 1½ quarts salmonberries, blueberries, or blackberries

Cream the shortening and sugar until fluffy. Add a little of the berry juice to make the mixture easier to beat, if you wish. Add the berries, a small amount at a time, until thoroughly mixed. Serve with smoked salmon strip.

MAKES 6 TO 8 SERVINGS

TIYULIK

12 trout livers (or 6 salmon livers)

2½ quarts crowberries or other berries

Clean the livers thoroughly and put to boil with a little water for 10 minutes. Remove from heat and cool. Mash the livers with a fork and add a little of the broth to make a smooth consistency. Add the berries and mix well. Tiyulik is rich in iron and vitamins A, D, and C.

MAKES 6 TO 8 SERVINGS

PEMMICAN "C"

1 pound animal fat

1 pound dried game meat

1 cup dried serviceberries, blueberries, or crowberries

½ cup dried rose hips

Cut the fat into small pieces and cook in a skillet over low heat until rendered. Discard any lumps. Put the dried meat in a bowl and pour over the liquid fat, then stir in the dried berries and rose hips. Set aside until fat has congealed.

Transfer the mixture to a large board and pound with a wooden mallet until the mixture is reduced to a pulpy mass about the consistency of ground beef. Shape the mass into small bars; roll up each bar in plastic wrap. Place the bars in plastic bags, several to a bag, and store in a cool, dry place, or freeze until needed. This sustaining trail food is rich in vitamin C.

SERVINGS VARY

In Norway, rose hips are dried and sold in powdered form and are used in many ways. You can dry and powder your own in order to have vitamin C all winter. There is not nearly as much vitamin as in the fresh rose hip, but a lot is retained when dried or otherwise processed.

BERRY GLOSSARY

CLOUDBERRY (*also known as lowbush salmonberry, aqpik, baked apple berry*): The cloudberry looks like a golden raspberry but rounder, with larger drupelets. As they ripen, their color lightens to a rose-peach shade. They have a juicy, tart taste and are high in vitamin C. Harvest the cloudberry in mid- to late summer, around August and September, when the berries are ripe and soft.

CROWBERRY (*also known as blackberry, mossberry*): Growing from small, evergreen shrubs, the crowberry resembles the blueberry in color and shape, though the crowberry is larger in size. Most people don't eat these raw as they can taste bitter and acidic, but the crowberry is great in syrups, jellies, and pies. Harvest after the first frost, around August and September, for a sweeter flavor, but be careful when you pick them as they are softer and burst more easily then.

CURRANT: Currants grow in clusters, their berries hanging from small branches with five-lobed, toothed leaves. The red currant is bright red and translucent while the black currant is more black and blue. Fresh currants have a rich but sour taste, though most prefer them in jams and jellies for their color and tart, sweet flavor. Harvest the currant in mid- to late summer, around July to August.

HIGHBUSH CRANBERRY: Not actually a true cranberry but related to the elderberry, the highbush cranberry is a vivid red, sometimes orange, fruit that grows on tall shrubs, with three-lobed leaves and small white flower clusters. This berry contains more water content than the lowbush cranberry and has a large seed in the middle. Sweeter than the lowbush cranberry, the highbush cranberry still has a musty, tart taste. Harvest in the summer, around August, when the berry is still hard and just before truly ripe for a better flavor, though it can be picked as late as September.

HUCKLEBERRY: Commonly confused with the blueberry, the huckleberry is roughly the same size but can be a shiny red, deep purple, or black, turning darker as it ripens on the stem. The red huckleberry has a tarter flavor while the black huckleberry is sweeter, but both are very juicy. Harvest in late summer, from August to September.

LOWBUSH CRANBERRY (*also known as lingonberry, cowberry*): The lowbush cranberry is a small, red fruit grown from shrubs with shiny green leaves and pink, bell-shaped flowers. Smaller than the cranberry, the lowbush cranberry also has a sweet, tart taste. Harvest in late fall after the first frost, around August to October.

MOUNTAIN ASH BERRY (*also known as Sitka mountain ash, western mountain ash, rowan berry*): This berry comes from a red-barked shrub with small clusters of white flowers, and can be a red or orange-red color. It has a sharp, unpleasant tart taste when eaten raw, but more often it's used dried or in jams and jellies. Harvest after the first frost, around August and September.

NAGOONBERRY (*also known as wineberry, Arctic raspberry, Arctic bramble*): The nagoonberry plant has red flowers and three-lobed, sharp-toothed leaves, and it produces jewel-red berries that resemble the raspberry but are deeper in color. The berry's taste is also reminiscent of a raspberry, being tart and sweet. Harvest in late summer, from August to September.

ROSE HIP (*also known as rose haw, rose hep*): The fruit of the rose plant, rose hips come in red, orange, purple, and even black colors. They're tart and tangy, and are high in vitamin C. Harvest after the first frost, around late August until October.

SALMONBERRY: The salmonberry grows from a shrub with pink-purple flowers and sharp-toothed leaves. The fruit looks like a large raspberry and come in yellow, orange, and red colors. Juicy when ripe, the salmonberry tastes tart and sweet and has lots of seeds. Harvest in mid- to late summer, from June to August, but be careful because they're fragile.

SERVICEBERRY (*also known as sarvisberry, shadbush, shadblow, juneberry, Saskatoon berry*): Grown from a tree or bush with white flowers and rounded, toothed leaves, the serviceberry is a small, purple-black berry with a sweet, almond flavor. Harvest in spring or summer, from May to July.

SOOPOLALLIE (*also known as soapberry, buffaloberry*): The soopolallie is a small, bright orange-red fruit grown from a woody shrub with dark green leaves. It has a juicy but bitter taste and can be soapy to the touch. Harvest in summer, from late July to August.

THIMBLEBERRY: The thimbleberry plant is a dense shrub with white, five-petaled flowers and big, toothed leaves. When ripe, the thimbleberry is a bright red fruit that resembles a raspberry, and is about the size and shape of a thimble. It has a sweet, sour taste and is full of many small seeds. Harvest when they're ripe and tender, around July to September.

WATERMELON BERRY (*also known as twisted stalk, wild cucumber*): As part of the lily family, the watermelon berry's plant has leaves like a lily's and bell-shaped white flowers. The stems have a unique, kinked look to them, which is where the name of the berry comes from. The berry itself is a deep red color and has lots of seeds, with a sweet flavor that people have compared to watermelons. The leaves and shoots, however, have a cucumberlike taste. Harvest the berry in summer, around July and August.

CANNING AND PRESERVING BERRIES

CLEANING BERRIES

A wet towel, placed over a slanted board with a large container such as a plastic dishpan at the bottom, makes an excellent berry cleaner. It is especially good for firm fruits like cranberries and blueberries. Simply pour the berries onto the top of the incline slowly and allow them to roll down and into the container at the bottom. Most debris—such as twigs, leaves, and the like—will stick to the damp towel. It doesn't get all the extraneous matter, but you won't need to do much more picking over.

CANNING IN GENERAL

Wild berries may be safely processed using the water bath method. If you have a pressure canner, it would be good to have the pressure gauge checked before starting your canning season. These gauges can sometimes be off by several pounds. Be sure all your canning equipment is thoroughly cleaned. Even though the equipment may be clean when it was put away the last time you used it, it does accumulate dirt even in storage.

Any large metal container should serve well for a boiling water bath canner. In days long gone by, we used to use an old-fashioned copper wash boiler for a canner. We fitted it with a homemade wooden rack. Check all glass jars and lids and discard any imperfect ones such as those dented, cracked, or chipped. Imperfections can cause imperfect sealing and thus cause spoilage of the fruit. Glass jars must be washed in hot, soapy water and well rinsed before using, even if they were put away clean after their last use. Wash them just before using.

Likewise, wash and rinse all lids. Heat the clean jars and lids in clean water before packing with hot fruit. Be sure to follow manufacturer's instructions. Rubber rings, if used, should be clean and new.

Tin cans and lids must be in perfect condition. Discard any dented, bent, or rusty cans and lids with damaged gaskets. Just before using, wash cans in clean water and turn upside down to drain. Washing lids may damage the gaskets, so they should be left in paper wrapping until the last minute, when they may be wiped with a damp cloth.

Test the can sealer before using. To do this, put a little water into a test can, seal it, and dunk in boiling water for a few seconds. If bubbles rise from the can, the seal is not tight. Follow the manufacturer's directions to adjust the sealer.

Always select fresh, firm berries for canning and can quickly as they tend to lose their freshness rapidly. Wash the berries if needed. This should not be necessary with fruit gathered away from dusty places. However, dirt often contains harmful bacteria, so if in doubt, wash. Don't allow the berries to soak but rinse them quickly in several changes of water. Always handle the fruit gently to avoid bruising.

Berries may be raw packed or hot packed (preheated and packed hot). Raw fruit needs to be packed in quite tightly because processing will cause it to shrink. Hot berries should be at, or near, boiling point when packed and may be packed more loosely.

There should be enough liquid (syrup, juice, or water) to fill in the space around the berries and to completely cover them. To remove air

bubbles from filled jars, simply slide a table knife blade down the sides in several places. Then add more liquid if needed to cover the fruit, but leave a little headspace at the top. Be sure to wipe rims of jars before putting on sealing lids. Some juice may have been spilled during the filling. Follow the manufacturer's directions exactly.

Tin cans must be "exhausted" before sealing raw fruit. Hot fruit may be sealed if you are sure the temperature has not gone below 170°F. To make sure, test with a thermometer, thrusting the bulb into the center of the can. To exhaust, place filled, open cans on a rack in a kettle in which there is enough boiling water to come about 2 inches below the can tops. Cover the kettle and bring the water to boiling. Boil until the thermometer inserted in the middle of a can registers 170°F. Remove the cans from the boiling water one at a time and add boiling packing liquid as needed to give the correct headspace. Put clean lids on the cans and seal at once.

Complete sealing of glass jars is necessary as they are taken from the hot water bath. If some liquid boiled away during processing, do not open jars to add more. Seal it just as it is. Cool with top side up, on folded cloth or rack; never set on cold surface and do not allow drafts to reach hot jars. However, never slow the cooling by covering the jars.

Tin cans should be immediately immersed in cold water to cool them. Change the water as needed for rapid cooling. Remove cans from water when they are still slightly warm and finish cooling and drying in the air. Air should be able to reach all cans, so it is good to stagger them

in the stack until they are completely cooled.

The next day, test the seal on each canning jar by turning the jar partly over in your hands. If you find a leaky jar, use the contents at once. Before storing canned berries, wipe the entire container with a damp cloth to remove any spilled fruit or juice. Label to show contents and date. Canned fruit should be stored in a cool, dry place.

PROCESSING IN BOILING WATER BATH

Put filled glass jars or tin cans into a canning vessel of hot or boiling water. For raw berries packed in glass, have water in canner hot but not boiling. For all other types of packing, use boiling water.

Add boiling water if needed to bring water an inch or so over tops of containers. Be careful not to pour the boiling water directly onto the glass jars. Cover the canning vessel.

When the water in the canner comes to a full rolling boil, start to count the number of minutes needed for processing. Boil gently and continuously for the recommended time. Remove containers immediately when processing time is up.

One minute additional boiling time is needed for each 1,000 feet above sea level. At 1,000 feet, add 1 minute to processing time. At 2,000 feet, add 2 minutes, and at 3,000 feet, add 3 minutes. Four minutes is right for 4,000-feet elevation.

To can berries with the raw pack method, clean and drain the fruit. Fill glass jars within ½ inch of the top, shaking berries down as you fill the jars. Cover with boiling syrup, leaving ½ inch headspace at the top. Adjust the lids and process in boiling water bath. Pint jars should be processed for 10 minutes and quarts for 15 minutes. Complete the seal as soon as jars are removed from the canner if they are not of the self-sealing type. In tin cans, fill to ¼ inch from top, shaking down the berries as you fill the cans. Fill to the top with boiling syrup. Exhaust to 170°F for 10 minutes and seal the cans. Process in a boiling water bath for 15 minutes for No. 2 cans or 15 minutes for No. 2½ cans.

To can berries with the hot pack method, be sure to use firm berries. Clean and drain if necessary. Add ½ cup sugar to each quart of berries. Cover the saucepan and bring to a boil, shaking the pan to keep fruit from sticking. Pack hot berries in glass jars to ½ inch from the top and adjust the jar lids. Process in a boiling water bath for 10 minutes for pints and 15 minutes for quarts. Complete seal as soon as jars are removed from the canner if closures are not self-sealing. In tin cans, you will need to pack the hot berries to the top. Exhaust for 10 minutes at 170°F. Seal cans and process in a boiling water bath. Process No. 2 cans for 15 minutes and No. 2-½ cans for 20 minutes.

To can berry juice, heat the juice to simmering. Strain through a wet jelly bag or other cloth. If sweet juice is desired, add from 1 to 1½ cups of sugar to each gallon of juice. Fill glass jars to almost the top with the hot juice. Adjust lids and process in a boiling water bath for 5 minutes for either pints or quarts. Remove the jars from canner and complete the seal. If you are using tin cans, fill to the top with the hot juice and seal at once. Process in the boiling water bath for 5 minutes for both No. 2 and No. 2½ cans.

For canning berry purees, simmer crushed fruit with a little water to keep from sticking. If the fruit is juicy, it may not be necessary to add any water but stir the pulp frequently to prevent sticking in any case. Put through a strainer or food mill and add sugar to taste. Heat again to the simmer point. Pack while still hot in glass jars to within ½ inch of the top. Adjust lids and process in a boiling water bath for 10 minutes for either pint or quart jars. Complete seals, if necessary, as soon as jars are removed from water. Or, pack to the top in tin cans and exhaust at 170°F for 10 minutes and seal cans. Process in boiling water bath for 10 minutes for either pints or quarts.

SWEETENING BERRIES

Sweetening helps canned berries hold their shape and retain their natural color and flavor. Very juicy berries, packed hot, can have sugar added without adding liquid. Sugar syrup may be used for many berries. Use the type of syrup that suits your taste.

Bring required amounts of sugar and water to a boil and boil gently for 5 minutes. Use as a canning or freezing syrup or as sweetener for beverages.

Type of Syrup	Sugar	Water	Yield
Thin	1 cup	2 cups	2½ cups
Medium thin	1 cup	1½ cups	2 cups
Medium	1 cup	1 cup	1½ cups
Heavy	1 cup	¾ cup	1¼ cups

Recipe may be doubled or tripled as needed. Yield is approximate. Fruit juice may be substituted for water if desired.

SUGAR ADDED DIRECTLY TO BERRIES

For juicy fruit to be hot packed, add ½ cup sugar to each quart of raw berries. Heat to simmering over low heat. Pack berries in the containers and pour the juice over them, leaving headspace.

SWEETENERS WITHOUT SUGAR

Light corn syrup or mild-flavored honey can be used to replace half of the sugar called for. Do not use brown sugar, sorghum, or molasses. Granulated sugar can be substituted if you wish; use ½ cup of the replacement to 4 cups of water. Bring to a boil and boil gently for 5 minutes. This makes a thin syrup with fewer calories.

UNSWEETENED FRUIT

Unsweetened berries can be canned in their own juice, in extracted juice, or in water. Thus canned, berries will not spoil but may be less colorful and may lose some of their flavor. Process as for sweetened berries.

TESTING FRUIT JUICE FOR PECTIN

If you are stuck wondering if the berries you have picked have enough natural pectin to jell, test their juice by either of these 2 simple methods provided by Robbie Jayne Johnson of Anchorage, Alaska:

METHOD 1: To 1 teaspoon of cooked juice, add 1 teaspoon of grain alcohol and stir slowly. You can discover the berries' natural jelling ability by keeping three principles in mind:

- Juices rich in pectin will form a large amount of bulky, gelatinous material.
- Juices moderately rich in pectin will form a few pieces of gelatinous material.
- Juices poor in pectin will form small, flaky pieces of sediment.

METHOD 2: Mix 2 teaspoons sugar, 1 tablespoon Epsom salts, and 2 tablespoons cooked juice. Stir well and let stand for 20 minutes. If the mixture forms a semi-solid mass, the juice contains sufficient pectin to jell.

THE SHEET TEST FOR JELLY

If you do not have a jelly thermometer to tell you when the boiling juice has reached the jelly stage, use the "sheet" test instead. Dip a cold, metal spoon into the boiling liquid and then hold it 12 to 18 inches above the pan but out of the path of rising steam. Turn the spoon so the jelly runs off the edge. If 2 or more drops form and run together before dripping off the edge of the spoon as separate drops, the jelly stage has been reached. It usually takes from 8 to 15 minutes to reach the sheet or jelly stage.

FREEZING BERRIES

Berries must be in top condition for freezing well. Do not use underripe or overripe fruit or any that is beginning to spoil. This means picking over the berries carefully and discarding unsuitable fruit. Work rapidly when preparing berries for the freezer. Have all needed supplies gathered and ready before berries are prepared to ensure getting the fruit into the freezer without undue delay.

CONTAINERS FOR BERRY FREEZING

Used milk cartons and glass containers are not recommended for containing frozen berries. For dry pack, plastic freezer bags are good. The little sandwich bags are not strong enough, so be sure to use a sturdier bag. Flexible or rigid plastic containers with lids are excellent, particularly if the square ones are used which fit together well and waste little space in storage. Round containers can be used, but they waste freezer space.

FREEZING IN QUANTITY

Clean blueberries or lowbush cranberries and spread on baking sheets or heavy-duty foil trays. Be sure they are dry and do not cling together. Then place in freezer and freeze until they are hard. Empty into a fair-sized plastic bag and close it airtight. You can freeze a big bag full of these, and they will remain separated from each other. When you want a few, just open the bag and take out the amount needed. Replace the bag in the freezer without thawing for use later on. This is the same way we now buy some frozen fruits and vegetables in the market. Just be sure you don't leave the berries on the baking sheets too long after they are frozen or they will become dehydrated. They need to be kept airtight.

LEAVE SOME IN THE FREEZER

Don't preserve all your frozen fruit. Leave some for use in breads, cookies, meat dishes, and other goodies, during the winter. It is especially nice to have a few lowbush cranberries to dip into when you want to make a loaf of Cranberry Nut Bread (page 23). Any that are left over you can always make into jam or something else before the new crop comes on.

FREEZING OUTDOORS

Lowbush cranberries, blueberries, and huckleberries may be stored out of doors to freeze if you live in the right climate for it. Clean berries and be sure there are no imperfect or overripe berries. If you have a mesh bag such as onions once were sold in, you are in luck. Otherwise improvise by using an old pillowcase or other cloth bag. It is essential that the berries get air circulation, so don't use plastic or other such bags. Perhaps you could use several thicknesses of cheesecloth to make a bag. One thickness is not strong enough. Do not put more than a couple quarts of the berries in one bag. Hang them up out of doors (under the eaves of the house, perhaps) within easy reach. You don't want to wade through deep snow to reach them later on. The berries will stay in excellent condition as long as the weatherman provides freezing temperatures, a long time in some parts of Alaska!

THAWING FROZEN BERRIES

Thaw berries in unopened containers at room

BERRY FREEZING CHART

BERRIES	SELECTION	PREPARATION	SAFE LIFE OF BERRIES IN FREEZER
Blueberries, all species	Firm, ripe berries	Wash in very cold water and scald in steam for one minute. Put in cold water to chill quickly. Dry pack.	18 months
Lowbush Cranberries	Firm, ripe berries	Wash only if necessary. No sugar or syrup needed. Dry pack.	24 months
Red Currants	Firm, good color	Wash only if needed and remove stems. One cup sugar to each three cups currants.	9 months
Other Currants		Not recommended for freezing	
Raspberries	Firm, ripe, perfect	Do not wash unless absolutely necessary; handle carefully. Pack dry or with one cup sugar to four cups berries.	9 months
Salmonberries, Cloudberries, Nagoonberries, and similar berries		Handled the same as raspberries	9 months
Gooseberries	Firm, ripe, good color	Wash if needed. Crush slightly to stimulate juice. One cup sugar to three cups berries.	9 months
Strawberries	Firm, ripe, perfect	Prepare as soon after gathering as possible as strawberries lose their flavor rapidly. Hull but do not wash unless really needed. Pack dry or use ½ cup sugar to four cups of fruit.	9 months
Rose Hips	Ripe, pick just before first frost	Clean and remove seeds with tip of knife. See recipe for Rose Hip Juice (page 160). Freezer containers instead of jars.	6 months
Highbush Cranberries		Not recommended for freezing	
Huckleberries		Same as for blueberries	18 months
Crowberries		Same as for blueberries	12 months
Serviceberries		Same as for blueberries	12 months
Salal		Same as for blueberries	12 months

temperature. All fruits tend to darken and lose flavor once they are thawed, so use them as soon as possible after thawing.

Fruits meant for a frozen dessert are best left slightly frozen as cream or sauce hastens the thawing.

Berries to be used in pies or cobblers or similar dishes need to be defrosted only enough to separate the fruit.

No thawing is necessary if berries are to be cooked in sauces, jam, preserves, and the like.

TIPS FOR FREEZING BERRIES

- Dead ripe fruit that is too ripe for normal freezing can be made into a puree by crushing in a kettle. Add a small amount of water and bring to the boiling point. Cook slowly for 5 minutes. Press the berries through a sieve or strainer. Package in freezer containers with ½ cup sugar to each 4 cups of puree and freeze as soon as puree is completely cold.
- Fruit juices may be frozen satisfactorily if you have room in your freezer. Simmer berries with just enough water to keep from sticking, for about 5 minutes. Extract the juice by pouring hot fruit into a wet jelly bag and allowing to drain for several hours or overnight. Do not squeeze bag as that will make the juice cloudy instead of clear. When juice is cold, package in freezer containers and freeze.
- Skins of blueberries and huckleberries tend to toughen in freezing. That is why these berries should be blanched with steam or by placing berries in a colander and lowered into boiling water for 1 minute.

- Always put containers of wild berries in the freezer as soon as prepared. Otherwise hold them in the refrigerator until you can put them in the freezer. Quick freezing is mandatory for berries.
- Always leave a little headspace in your freezer container—half an inch is enough.
- Be sure to label and indicate the date of freezing so that you can control your frozen berry inventory.
- Be sure to clean berries well before freezing; see page 188 and 195 for instructions.
- To freeze whole berries rapidly, arrange them on a paper towel-lined baking sheet with a little bit of space around each berry. Place the baking sheet in the freezer and freeze until firm, a couple of hours or up to 1 day. Transfer the frozen berries to freezer containers for longer storage.
- Properly stored, frozen berries should last for up to a year or more.

DRYING BERRIES

Drying wild berries is a great project for those who live in the bush or elsewhere far from supermarkets. It is reported that when dried, berries retain much of their nutritional value too.

CHECKING BERRIES FOR DRYING

Berries with thick or tough skins, such as blueberries, serviceberries, and crowberries, should be checked before attempting to dry. Otherwise only the skin will dry and the inside of the berry will remain moist. Checking is accomplished by placing a small amount of the berries at a time in a colander (or cloth bag) and dunking in boiling water for one minute. Drain thoroughly as the berries should harbor no excess moisture before being spread to dry.

BASIC WAYS TO PREPARE BERRIES FOR DRYING

There are two basic ways to dry our wild berries. They may be dried whole or they may be first made into a puree which can then be dried. Those that have small seeds respond well to the first method. Large-seeded fruit, such as rose hips or highbush cranberries, are best seeded first or else dried by the puree method.

DRYING BERRIES BY OTHER METHODS

It is possible to make your own dryer with several shelves for holding the berries as they dry. There are commercial dryers for home use on the market too. However, unless you plan to go into drying in a big way, the sun- or oven-dried methods will do well enough. The sun-dried fruit seems to have the best flavor; probably that is natural.

OVEN-DRIED BERRIES Whole berries may also be dried in the oven. Set the oven at lowest heat. Line a baking sheet with a single layer of paper towels and thinly spread out the berries. Put in the oven and leave the oven door ajar a bit. You may need to prop the door open with a pencil or a small stick. This is done to allow moisture to escape and to keep the berries drying slowly. They are to be dried and not cooked.

PUREE METHOD OF DRYING BERRIES

Place berries in a saucepan with a small amount of water. If they are quite juicy, no water will be required. Stir over low heat until the berries are soft. Put them through a sieve or food mill to obtain a smooth paste or puree. The puree is then spread thinly on sheets of waxed paper. They can be either dried out of doors in the sun or oven dried as with whole berries. When completely dry, the puree may be broken into small chunks or chips and put in plastic bags to store in the freezer.

STORING DRIED BERRIES

Dried berries should be stored in a cool dry place. They can be put up in plastic bags or stored in screw-top jars. It is a good idea to inspect dried fruit occasionally since sometimes they become a bit moldy if they were not dried thoroughly enough.

USING DRIED BERRIES

Whole dried berries may be used like raisins or commercially dried currants; or they may be reconstituted by adding a little water and allowing to soak for an hour or so, then simmering gently for a few minutes before using. The puree may be reconstituted in similar fashion. It can also be crushed with a rolling pin and added to puddings, pies, and other berry dishes.

ROSE HIP POWDER

Rose hip powder may be made by crushing dried puree with a rolling pin until it is fine enough to suit you. This may be stored in small jars in a cool, dry place. It is good to sprinkle over cereal and to include in hot cakes and other dishes to give vitamin C as needed. The dry rose hips lose some of their vitamin content; still, they retain a lot, which makes up for their comparative lack of flavor.

INDEX

Originally published as *Alaska Wildberry Guide & Cookbook* © 1982, *The Alaska Wild Berry Cookbook* © 2012 Alaska Northwest Books

Library of Congress Cataloging-in-Publication Data is on file

ISBN 9781513261195 (paperback)
ISBN 9781513261201 (hardbound)
ISBN 9781513261218 (e-book)

Printed in China
25 24 23 22 5 6 7 8

Recipe Editor: Kristen Tate
Indexer: Elizabeth Parson

Alaska Northwest Books®
An imprint of

WEST
MARGIN
PRESS

WestMarginPress.com

Proudly distributed by Ingram Publisher Services

WEST MARGIN PRESS
Publishing Director: Jennifer Newens
Marketing Manager: Angela Zbornik
Editor: Olivia Ngai
Design & Production: Rachel Lopez Metzger